6/10

CULTURES OF THE WORLD
Cyprus

Michael and Jo-Ann Spilling

Marshall Cavendish
Benchmark
New York

PICTURE CREDITS

Cover: © Photononstop/SuperStock

AFP/Getty Images: 93 • Alex Mita/AFP/Getty Images: 54 • Andy Sotiriou/ Getty Images: 44 • Audrius Tomonis: 135 • David G. Houser: 26, 64, 98, 99, 103 • Dorota and Mariusz Jarymowicz/Getty Images: 2, 46 • Focus Team—Italy: 7, 14, 62, 72, 77, 113, 114, 122, 129 • Hutchison Library: 76 • Izzet Keribar/ Lonely Planet Images: 22 • Jens Lucking/ Getyy images: 11 • Jihan Ammar/AFP/Getty Images: 86 • Milos Bicanski/Stringer/ Getty Images: 36 • North Wind Picture Archives: 24 • Oliver Strewe/ Lonely Planet Images: 23 • Patrick Baz/AFP/ Getty Images: 38, 39 • photolibrary: 5, 6, 8, 9, 10, 13, 15, 16, 17, 19, 21, 27, 32, 35, 42, 43, 52, 53, 56, 63, 68, 78, 80, 83, 94, 96, 97, 104, 105, 106, 108, 109, 112, 118, 120, 121, 124, 125, 128, 130, 131 • STR/AFP/Getty Images: 34, 55 • Topham Picturepoint: 18, 50, 70, 74, 101, 117 • Trip Photolibrary: 12, 25, 29, 30, 48, 49, 65, 88, 92, 111, 115, 123, 127 • Veronica Garbutt/ Lonely Planet Images: 1, 60

PRECEDING PAGE

An elderly man from Limassol.

Publisher (U.S.): Michelle Bisson
Editors: Deborah Grahame, Stephanie Pee
Copyreader: Tara Tomczyk
Designers: Nancy Sabato, Steven Tan
Cover picture researcher: Connie Gardner
Picture researcher: Thomas Khoo

Marshall Cavendish Benchmark
99 White Plains Road
Tarrytown, NY 10591
Website: www.marshallcavendish.us

© Times Media Private Limited 2000
© Marshall Cavendish International (Asia) Private Limited 2010
All rights reserved. First edition 2000. Second edition 2010.
® "Cultures of the World" is a registered trademark of Times Publishing Limited.

Originated and designed by Times Media Private Limited
An imprint of Marshall Cavendish International (Asia) Private Limited
A member of Times Publishing Limited

Marshall Cavendish is a trademark of Times Publishing Limited.

All Internet sites were correct and accurate at the time of printing. All monetary figures in this publication are in U.S. dollars.

Library of Congress Cataloging-in-Publication Data
Spilling, Michael.
  Cyprus / by Michael Spilling and Jo-Ann Spilling. — 2nd ed.
    p. cm. — (Cultures of the world)
  Summary: "Provides comprehensive information on the geography, history, wildlife, governmental structure, economy, cultural diversity, peoples, religion, and culture of Cyprus"—Provided by publisher.
  Includes bibliographical references and index.
  ISBN 978-0-7614-4855-6
  1. Cyprus—Juvenile literature. I. Spilling, Jo-Ann. II. Title.
  DS54.A3S65 2010
  956.93—dc22   2009045689

Printed in China
9 8 7 6 5 4 3 2 1

CONTENTS

INTRODUCTION

CYPRUS IS AN ISLAND COUNTRY STRATEGICALLY SITUATED IN the eastern Mediterranean. This distinctive oval-shaped island with its "panhandle" northeast peninsula is the Mediterranean's third-largest island. Cyprus's history has been shaped and influenced by a range of different people and cultures, including the Greeks, Romans, Persians, Arabs, Byzantines, Crusaders, Turks, and British colonists. Today this beautiful island is one of Europe's most popular tourist destinations, receiving millions of visitors every year.

Cyprus became an independent republic on August 16, 1960. Ethnic tension has existed between the Greek Cypriots and Turkish Cypriots for many years. Following the Greek coup-d'etat and the Turkish invasion of Cyprus on July 20, 1974, Cyprus has been divided into the Republic of Cyprus in the south and the Turkish-occupied area in the north, also known as the Turkish Republic of Northern Cyprus (TRNC). Only the Republic of Cyprus is recognized by the international community. Since 1964, Cyprus has relied on the presence of the United Nations (UN) peacekeeping forces to maintain law and order. In spite of the country's turmoil, Cypriots are relaxed, hospitable people who are proud of their identity and traditions.

GEOGRAPHY

The coastline of Cyprus from Point Akamas.

Cyprus is the third-largest island in the Mediterranean, after Sardinia and Sicily.

THE ISLAND OF CYPRUS LIES IN the far eastern corner of the Mediterranean Sea, about 40 miles (64 kilometers) south of Turkey, 60 miles (97 km) west of Syria, and 480 miles (772 km) south of mainland Greece. The island is 140 miles (225 km) long from the northeastern tip of Cape Andreas to the western coast of Cape Arnauti, but only 60 miles (97 km) at its widest point from north to south. It has a total area of 3,571 square miles (9,250 square km).

Cyprus has four major topographical regions. The Kyrenia Mountains run along the northern coast, while the Troodos Mountains cover a larger area to the south and west. Between the two ranges lies the Mesaoria Plain. To the east and south of the Troodos Mountains are hills.

Politically Cyprus is divided into the Greek south and the Turkish north, a result of long-standing ethnic conflict and the 1974 Turkish invasion. The underpopulated northern area, the Turkish Republic of North Cyprus, makes up about 36 percent of the island. It includes the Kyrenia Mountains,

Right: A glimpse of the Troodos Mountains, the tallest in Cyprus.

most of the Mesaoria Plain (*Mesaoria* means "between the mountains" in Greek), the Karpas Peninsula, and the small enclave of Erenköy in the west. The larger, more prosperous Republic of Cyprus in the south consists of the Troodos Mountains and the extensive foothills toward the south and west of the mountains.

MOUNTAINS AND PLAINS

Cyprus has two major mountain ranges—the Troodos, formed from molten rock beneath the ocean, and the Kyrenia, part of the Alpine-Himalayan chain that runs through the Eastern Mediterranean.

The Troodos Mountains stretch from the northwest coast for about 50 miles (80 km) to Stavrovouni Peak (2,260 feet / 689 meters), which lies about 12 miles (19 km) from the southern coast. At 6,401 feet (1,951 m), Mount Olympus, sometimes known as Mount Troodos, is Cyprus's highest peak. On a clear winter day, there is a fantastic view from the northern slopes of Mount

The Troodos Mountains are one of two mountain ranges in Cyprus.

Workers harvesting potatoes in the Larnaka district in southern Cyprus.

Olympus across Morphou Bay to the faraway Toros Mountains in Turkey. In contrast to the Kyrenia Mountains, the foothills and valleys of the Troodos Mountains are undulating and spacious. Two of the most beautiful valleys are the Marathasa and Soleas, which cut into the northern slopes of the range. The valleys and folds of the hills conceal a huge number of villages, the highest of which is Prodromos, at 4,600 feet (1,402 m) above sea level.

Hugging the northern coast of Cyprus is the narrow, 100-mile-long (161-km-long) Kyrenia Mountains, which are also known as the Pentadaktylos ("five-fingered") Range.

Lying between the two mountain ranges is the flat, low-lying Mesaoria Plain, which stretches from the city of Famagusta on the east coast to Morphou Bay in the west. In the center of the plain lies Nicosia, which is the capital of Cyprus. Dubbed the breadbasket of Cyprus, the Mesaoria Plain is the main cereal-growing area of the island, though only half of the land is irrigated.

The panhandle-shaped area of northeastern Cyprus is known as the Karpas Peninsula. The peninsula is remote and unspoiled, and it is an unpolluted, rich source of marine and bird life.

RIVERS AND LAKES

All of the island's major rivers originate in the Troodos Mountains. The largest, the Pedhieos, flows east toward Famagusta Bay. Along with the Yialias, it irrigates much of the Mesaoria Plain. Other major rivers include the Karyoti, which flows north to Morphou Bay, and the Kouris, which flows south toward Episkopi Bay. Much of Cyprus's distinctive appearance comes from the valleys created by these rivers with their deep, gravel beds. All the rivers, which are dry in the summer months, rely on winter rainfall. However, during sudden summer thunderstorms, some of the *wadis* (the Arabic term for "valleys") can turn into raging torrents in under an hour.

Larnaka Salt Lake, with the Hala Sultan Tekke Mosque in the background.

Mount Olympus is covered in snow from January to March.

On the south coast, two large saltwater lakes have formed near the towns of Limassol and Larnaca. These lagoons are a rich habitat for bird life, particularly in December and April, when birds migrate between Europe and the Nile Delta.

CLIMATE

Cyprus has an intense Mediterranean climate marked by strong seasonal differences. Summer lasts from June to September, while winter lasts from November to March. Spring and autumn are short and are characterized by rapid changes in climate and an equally fast transformation of local plant life. Summers are hot and dry, but not humid. The central plain is usually the hottest, with temperatures averaging 99°F (37°C) in Nicosia. Winters are mild, and the weather varies, with average temperatures a cool 41—59°F (5—15°C). The higher reaches of the Troodos Mountains experience several weeks of below-freezing nighttime temperatures in the winter. Rain generally occurs

Prickly pear found on the north coast of Cyprus.

between October and March, with average annual rainfall of about 20 inches (51 centimeters). The island's agriculture is dependent on this rainfall, which is often unreliable. The mountain areas receive far more rain than the Mesaoria Plain. Average annual rainfall in Nicosia, for example, is only 14 inches (36 cm), while in the Troodos Mountains, it can be nearly 40 inches (102 cm). Over the past 30 years, rainfall levels have been decreasing in Cyprus.

FLORA

As one of the island's major natural resources, the forests of Cyprus have been extensively exploited for many centuries. This has occurred partly for economic reasons, because the local people needed wood for export and land for farming. At one time both the plains and mountains of Cyprus were forested. Today only 10 percent of the island is still covered in forest. As early as 400 B.C., the island's rulers placed the local cedar forests under protection, but despite this, the island's forests have continued to be plundered by both conquerors and locals alike. Today the remaining forests are high in the Troodos and Kyrenia mountain ranges. Recently the forestry department tried to stop the loss of forests with extensive replanting but these efforts have not yet been implemented.

The most common tree of the Troodos range is the Aleppo pine, which makes up 90 percent of all forests in Cyprus. In the upper reaches of the mountains, black pine can also be found. The pine forests are hardy and can resist the extremes of heat and cold. In the Troodos valleys, golden oak, and willow can be found. As on many Mediterranean islands, cypress, eucalyptus, and juniper trees are common. The most famous tree in Cyprus is the cedar. However, today cedar trees only grow within the Paphos forest on the slopes of Mount Tripylos, in the southwest area of the island.

BLOOMING CYPRUS

Cyprus is one of the best places in Europe to see flowers. The island's 1,800 species of flowering plants are characteristic of both Asia Minor and the Mediterranean. They include 170 species of grasses and 90 species of carnation. In April, the height of spring in Cyprus, the island is a blaze of color. Pink oleander is common and grows all over Cyprus along roadsides and highways.

There are 125 species of flowers that can only be found in Cyprus. These include the dark red tulip or Tulipa Cypria, and the pinkish-white meadow saffron, Colchicum Troodi. The meadow saffron can be found from the Troodos Mountains right down to the coast. Local carnations include Silene, Petrorhagia, Dianthus, and Arenaria. The best month to appreciate the flora of the Troodos Mountains is May. As soon as the snow melts, flowers such as violets, forget-me-nots, veronicas, and crocuses start to bloom. In the lowland areas, wood daisies, Bermuda buttercups, wild cyclamens, and spiny burnets thrive. Orchids are one of the island's most common plants. So far 44 different species or subspecies, as well as many hybrids, have been discovered. Examples include the pyramid orchid, the small-leafed helleborine orchid, the buffoon orchid, the Anatolian orchid, and the bee orchid, all of which can also be found in Greece and Turkey. In addition, Cyprus has a number of insect orchids, which get their name because their flowers look like insects. The rare dotted orchid, with its red and yellow flowers, can also be found in Cyprus. Orchids mainly grow in the Kyrenia Mountains and limestone areas around the Troodos range. All in all, Cyprus is a botanist's delight.

Extensive scrub covers the foothills and low-lying areas that are not under cultivation. The scrub is made up of bulky, thorny bushes. The mastic shrub is very common, as are the turpentine tree and the strawberry tree. Rock rose bushes grow over the dry, sun-drenched hills, and can even be found on slopes high in the Kyrenia range. The southern and western slopes of the Troodos are extensively planted with grapevines, while orange groves dominate the area around Morphou Bay. Other cultivated trees include olive, carob, walnut, lemon, grapefruit, fig, date palm, and pomegranate. The Akamas Peninsula is home to more than 500 species of plants, including Aleppo pines, cypress, Phoenician junipers, and carob, oak, and caper trees.

FAUNA

Domestic animals, such as donkeys and oxen, are still a part of village life, and are used for pulling carts and plows. Wild donkeys also roam the Karpas Peninsula. However, wild animals are now rare. The only large wild animal still

Pine trees are a well-known feature of the eastern Mediterranean.

Donkeys are still an integral part of village life in Cyprus.

living in Cyprus is the agrino, a kind of wild sheep. It is under strict protection in a small forested area of the Troodos range. This rare animal has become a symbol of Cyprus. Small game is abundant but aggressively hunted, and foxes, hedgehogs, and shrews can be found all over the island. In contrast to much of the Mediterranean, sheep and goats are rare.

In classical times, snakes were so common that the island was named *Orphiussa*, which means "the abode of snakes." Now snakes are relatively rare. North of Paphos, the beaches of Cape Lara have become famous for nesting loggerhead turtles, a rare, protected species. The sandy beaches of the Karpas Peninsula provide nesting grounds for loggerhead turtles. Cyprus is home to many lizards because its high temperatures and dry climate provide an ideal environment for them. The country's lizards include the impressive starred agama, which grows to a length of 12 inches (30 cm). It lives in rocky crevices and stone walls. The southern slopes of the Kyrenia Mountains are home to the blunt-nosed viper, and climbers occasionally have unwelcome encounters with these ledge-dwelling reptiles. Chameleons also live in Cyprus.

The western coast of the Paphos district is one of the last nesting grounds in the Mediterranean for green and loggerhead turtles, both of which are endangered species. The turtles require dry land to lay their eggs, so they choose deserted, sandy beaches for this purpose. In Cyprus the turtles nest every two to three years from early June to mid-August. Each turtle lays about 100 eggs every two weeks. The eggs are buried about 20 inches (51 cm) below the sand surface. The hatchlings emerge seven weeks later and instinctively dash for the sea, which they recognize from reflected moonlight or starlight. Sometimes artificial lights from taverns, hotels, and flashlights distract the newborn turtles, causing them to move the wrong way and later die of dehydration. Tourist development has narrowed the choice of realistic breeding grounds for turtles, and popular nesting places such as Ayia Napa can no longer be used. Once in the water, the hatchlings are easy prey for seals, sharks, and other large fish. On land the eggs are sometimes dug up and eaten by foxes. As a result, it is estimated that only one in every 1,000 eggs develops into an adult. Sea turtles only reach maturity 15 to 30 years after hatching.

Surveys indicated an alarming drop in the turtle population, and in 1978, the Cypriot government set up a project around Cape Lara to try to reverse the decline. The beaches around Cape Lara are off-limits to tourists every summer, when volunteers search the beaches for eggs. If a nest is judged to be poorly sited, the eggs are dug up and moved to a better location with anti-fox wire mesh. The Lara project has yielded good results and has increased the yearly hatchling survival rate fourfold.

Bird life in Cyprus is varied and interesting. More than 350 different species of birds have been found on the island, most of which migrate. The remote and undeveloped Karpas Peninsula is a natural, unpolluted habitat for most of the island's birds, and along with the Akamas Peninsula on the west coast, it is one of the few wild places left in Cyprus. More than 160 bird species, 12 mammals, 20 reptiles, and 16 butterfly species have been identified in the Akamas area, including falcons, turtledoves, crested larks, the Cyprus warbler, and Scops's owl. Around the salt lakes of southern Cyprus, flamingos, herons, spoonbills, geese, and ducks can be seen. The salt lakes are an ideal habitat for brine shrimp, which make perfect food for flamingos. The Gönyeli reservoir, on the northern edge of Nicosia, is a good place to see migrating birds.

More northern species, such as pigeons, wagtails, blackbirds, finches, and larks, visit the island in winter. Rock rose warblers, whitethroats, blue rock thrush, coal tits, wrens, corn bunting, and sparrows are among the birds that nest in Cyprus. The rocky coastal crags of the Kyrenia Mountains are home to griffon vultures, hawks, peregrine falcons, and kestrels. The magnificent griffon vulture has a wingspan of 8 feet (2.5 m).

A pelican in Paphos, Cyprus.

TOWNS

Cypriots are traditionally rural people, and the village is the center of their lives. A steady drift of population to the towns began early in the 20th

The old city of Nicosia within the Venetian walls consists of narrow streets lined with houses, workshops, cafés, and stores.

century. This accelerated after the Turkish invasion of the island in 1974 and the consequent need to resettle many refugees in the southern part of the island. Before 1974 only six places were listed as towns—settlements of more than 5,000 people and 600 villages were recorded. These six towns—Nicosia, Limassol, Larnaca, Paphos, Famagusta, and Kyrenia—are the main urban settlements in Cyprus today. They are also the administrative centers for the island's six districts. One result of the Turkish invasion is that the southern, Greek portion of Cyprus is far more populated than the northern, Turkish area. Many of the Cypriots who fled to the south settled around the towns of Limassol, Larnaca, and Paphos, which have grown rapidly since. Nicosia, the capital, remains the only large inland settlement. It is rare for an island capital not to lie on the coast.

NICOSIA, the capital of Cyprus, is a divided city, with the northern portion occupied by Turks and the larger, southern section occupied by Greeks. The capital of Cyprus does not even have a common name—the Turks call it *Lefkosa*, while the Greeks call it *Lefkosia*. Nicosia is an old name that was given to the city by European conquerors. The city has been divided since 1964, when communal violence between Turks and Greeks caused the British to divide the city. Around 270,000 people live in the Greek portion of the city, while only 85,000 live in the Turkish section. Nicosia was founded in A.D. 965 by the Byzantine rulers of the island, but only rose to prominence as the administrative capital under Lusignan rule during the 12th to 15th centuries. The distinctive, circular wall of the city center with its 11 bastions dates from the time of Venetian rule, built between 1567 and 1570. The city contains many Greek churches and Muslim mosques, which is evidence of its variable, turbulent history.

LIMASSOL is a busy trading and tourist center and the island's busiest port. It has a natural harbor, and has been occupied by people since the Bronze Age. Limassol was a Byzantine settlement and later a center for the Crusades.

A container ship off the coast of Limassol, a busy trading center.

In Nicosia, United Nations (UN) peacekeeping forces guard the border crossing, while Greek and Turkish soldiers face one another across the "green line" (the United Nations buffer zone in Cyprus) that cuts the capital in two. The green line is a ceasefire line that was named after a British officer marked the dividing line between the Greek and Turkish sectors on a map with green ink in 1963.

The town did not expand into an important trading center until the late 19th century, when it came under British protection. After the 1974 invasion, the city doubled in size, taking in 45,000 Greek Cypriot refugees. Today it has a population of 176,900 and is the second-largest city on the island. It is estimated that one in three tourists who visit Cyprus spend time on the Bay of Amathus, just east of the town, where a six-mile (10-km) stretch of hotels and man-made beaches joins the town to the 3,000-year-old ruins of Amathus. This, combined with visitors from the nearby British army base, ensures that Limassol has a lively nightlife and cosmopolitan atmosphere.

LARNACA Farther east along the southern coast is Larnaca, Cyprus's third-largest town. Larnaca, which has a population of 125,700, reached its peak in the 19th century, when many international trading offices and consulates were based there for convenience. Since 1974 Larnaca has been the site of the island's international airport. To the east of Larnaca, the land is cramped, a consequence of the Turkish invasion and a demarcation line just to the north of the city. United Nations troops, Greek soldiers, and the many tourists who flock to this city give Larnaca an overcrowded appearance.

PAPHOS Situated on the southwest coast of the island, Paphos is a city with a truly glorious past. In ancient times the settlement was a place of pilgrimage throughout the Hellenic world as a center for fertility rituals. Later the small port became a Roman settlement. Paphos used to be a backward, undeveloped, sparsely populated area. However, this changed in 1982 when an airport was built to develop tourism. A new airport terminal opened in November 2008 adjacent to the old one. Now the city has a population of 67,400 and is increasingly popular with tourists.

FAMAGUSTA In the Turkish north, there are only two towns of significant size, Famagusta and Kyrenia. Founded by Ptolemy II in the third century B.C., Famagusta later fell to Arab conquerors, then became a Byzantine conquest in the 12th century A.D. During the Crusades, the town was a thriving center of East-West trade. Following the Ottoman conquest in 1570, no Christian subject was allowed to live within its walls. The new town of Varosha was established nearby for Christians who had been expelled from Famagusta. Before the Turkish invasion in 1972, Varosha was a tourist town. Today, however, it is a ghost town. Famagusta, like Limassol, has a natural harbor, but since the Turkish invasion in 1974, it is seldom used. Today Famagusta has a population of around 42,500.

KYRENIA Located on the northern coast, Kyrenia once known as the Jewel of the Levant because of its picturesque setting and cosmopolitan social life. Following the 1974 invasion, many Anatolian Turks from the mainland settled here. Today, Kyrenia is a tranquil coastal town with a population of 28,500. Most of Kyrenia dates from the medieval and Ottoman periods. It boasts of a beautiful harbor, a medieval castle, and a promenade with Venetian-style facades.

The city of Kyrenia.

HISTORY

Wildflowers and the ruins of Saint Hilarion Castle in northern Cyprus.

INVASION AND OUTSIDE DOMINATION have been the norm for 10,000 years of Cyprus's turbulent history. The powers that controlled the eastern Mediterranean sought to control Cyprus, an important stepping-stone to the Middle East and Asia Minor. Greeks, Persians, Romans, Arabs, and Turks have all left splendid monuments and ethnic diversity in their wake.

BEGINNINGS

Evidence of human habitation in Cyprus dates from the Neolithic period, before 6000 B.C. Excavations at Khirokitia suggest that there was a settlement of about 2,000 people, living in round stone houses. The community died out after a few centuries, and the island was uninhabited for 2,000 years. The next period of habitation, the Sotira culture, dates from 4500 B.C. The people lived by hunting and fishing. In the Copper Stone age, dating from 3000 to 2500 B.C., people made tools and pottery from copper.

During the late Bronze Age (1600—1200 B.C.), Cyprus became absorbed into the

Right: Remains of a neolithic village in Cyprus.

23

Hittite Empire and the island's contacts extended from the Aegean Sea to the Nile Delta. Mass immigration of Greek-speaking people from the Peloponnese occurred in the Iron Age (1100—700 B.C.), establishing the Greek language and six kingdoms on the island: Curium, Paphos, Marion, Soli, Lapithos, and Salamis. Around 800 B.C. a new Phoenician colony was established at Citium. This culture had a great influence on Cyprus.

GREEKS AND PERSIANS

In 709 B.C. the kingdoms of Cyprus submitted to Assyrian rule. Assyrian domination ended in 669 B.C., and after that, Cyprus enjoyed a century of independence and exuberant, artistic development. Later Egypt became dominant in the eastern Mediterranean and in 569 B.C. the Cypriot kings were forced to recognize the pharaoh Ahmose II as their ruler.

In 545 B.C. Cyprus was conquered by the Persians. The Persian expansion dragged Cyprus into a long war between the Greeks and the Persians. When

Naval victory of Greeks over Persians at Salamis.

the Ionians (a Greek people) revolted against Persian rule in 499 B.C., all the Cypriot kingdoms, except Amathus, joined the revolt. The revolt was suppressed after a year.

Greece and Persia continued to struggle for power in Cyprus. The island became an extremely important naval base in the eastern Mediterranean, and was valued for its supplies of wood for shipbuilding. King Evagoras I of Salamis succeeded in unifying the island under his rule, but he was assassinated in 374 B.C.

GREEKS AND ROMANS

After the swift conquest of the eastern Mediterranean by the Macedonian ruler Alexander the Great (356—323 B.C.), Cyprus willingly became part of his vast empire. After his death in 323 B.C., the island kingdoms fell into the hands of Ptolemy I of Egypt in 294 B.C., and the island was held by Egypt for the next 250 years.

In 58 B.C. Cyprus was annexed by the expanding Roman Republic. For the next 600 years, Cyprus enjoyed the peace and stability brought about by integration into the Roman and later, Byzantine Empire. The island's road network improved, and many public buildings were erected. The Roman garrison remained minimal, and Cypriots went about their affairs with little interference.

THE BYZANTINE EMPIRE

When the Roman Empire divided in A.D. 395, Cyprus remained a part of the Byzantine Empire. The Arabs under the leadership of Muawiya, who swept through the eastern Mediterranean in the seventh century, conquered the island in A.D. 649. In A.D. 688 a treaty between the Byzantine emperor Justinian II and the Arab ruler 'Abd al-Malik effectively freed Cyprus from direct Arab rule for 300 years, introducing an unstable period during which

A reconstructed Byzantine olive-oil press.

the island was forced to pay tribute to one or the other power, and sometimes both. Cyprus underwent great social changes during this time. There was an influx of Muslims and Arabs, and the island was constantly invaded by Arab forces and harassed by pirates. Many of the cities lay in permanent ruin. However, in A.D. 965, the Byzantine emperor Nicephorus II Phocas regained the island, and a period of economic and cultural prosperity followed.

THE LUSIGNAN KINGDOM

In 1185 the Byzantine governor of Cyprus, Isaac Comnenus, rebelled against Byzantium and declared himself emperor. However, he was defeated by King Richard I of England who was on his way to the Holy Land during the Third Crusade. Richard later sold the island to Guy of Lusignan, the Crusader king who had lost Jerusalem to Saladin, the sultan of Egypt's forces following the Crusader defeat at the Battle of Hattin in 1187.

Cyprus suffered a significant fall in population between 1570 and 1740—dropping from 200,000 people in 1570 to 120,000 by 1600, and 95,000 by 1740, following a number of natural disasters and further immigration.

Ayios Neophytos monastery is famous for its 12th-century frescoes.

The Buyuk Han, the Great Inn, was restored over a decade, from 1992 to 2002.

The Lusignan dynasty (1192—1489) ruled the island for the next 300 years, although economic competition led Venice and Genoa to get involved in Cypriot affairs. During the reign of Peter II (1369—82), both Genoa and Venice competed to control the island's valuable trade. Genoese troops seized Famagusta in 1374, and held it for the next 90 years. The last Lusignan king, Jacques II (reigned 1460 to 73), regained the throne and managed to expel the Genoese from Famagusta. His wife, Catarina Cornaro, succeeded him, but she ceded Cyprus to Venice during her reign (1474—89). Venice controlled Cyprus for 82 years.

OTTOMAN RULE

From the base of their power in the old Byzantine heartland in Turkey, the Ottomans grew in power during the 16th century, capturing Syria, Palestine, and Egypt. In 1570, 350 Turkish ships landed at Larnaca, and the island fell to the Ottomans the next year. Twenty thousand Turks settled on the island after the conquest, while most of the Latin inhabitants immigrated. For the next 300 years, Cyprus became a poor, undeveloped backwater of the Ottoman Empire.

One of the most significant consequences of Ottoman rule was a steady increase in the Turkish population. Turks made up 31 percent of the island's population by 1841. However, there was little mixing between Turks and Greeks, partly because of their different status under Ottoman rule, but mainly because of religious differences. A second significant development was the gradual increase in the power of the Orthodox Church. Under the Ottomans, religious leaders were assumed to have political power and responsibilities, making the Orthodox Church more and more powerful in the Greek community.

Nevertheless abuses of power and corruption were common. High taxes were levied in an arbitrary manner on both Greek and Turkish peasants. The rural population grew increasingly dissatisfied with their lot under the thumb of both Turkish rulers and wealthy Orthodox clergy. When the Greek nationalist uprising occurred on the Greek mainland in 1821, a backlash against Greek Cypriots resulted in massacres of local intellectuals and clergymen. Troops were brought in from Syria and Egypt, and a six-month reign of terror left many dead. This caused resentment among the Greeks and an increase in the nationalist feelings the massacres were intended to quell. Turkish envy rose because of Greek prosperity and higher levels of education. Many poorer rural Turks had become second-class citizens in a country they had conquered only a few hundred years before.

A BRITISH COLONY

The Greek war of liberation marked the beginning of the swift decline of the Ottoman Empire. British power extended through the eastern Mediterranean in the 19th century. Turkey's weakening power and the opening of the Suez Canal in 1869 gave the British more and more influence over the Turkish authorities. The Cyprus Convention of 1878 said that Britain would administer the island, which would remain under Turkish sovereignty. The agreement was seen as part of a deal in which the British would reinforce Turkish power against the increasing threat of Russian expansion in the Caucasus on Turkey's northern border. Britain wanted to make sure its trade route through the Suez Canal to India would be protected.

With the start of World War I and a declaration of hostilities between Turkey and Britain in 1914, Britain annexed the island. The island officially became a British colony in 1925. British rule brought increasing efficiency to the outmoded and corrupt administration of Cyprus. A modern education system was introduced, with separate schools for Christians and Muslims. Contact with Western Europe meant that Cypriot trade boomed for the first time in more than 300 years. A legislative council was formed, consisting of both Cypriots and the British, for making joint administrative decisions. However, British modernization only affected the cities; little change occurred in the villages. Taxes were high under British rule, and Britain invested little in developing the island's infrastructure.

Disillusionment with British rule and an increase in Greek nationalism led Greek Cypriots to demand to be united with the Greek motherland, which had become independent with the demise of the Ottoman Empire at the end of World War I. Such demands led to riots in Nicosia in 1931. During World War II, Cyprus was not directly involved in the fighting, and the island gained from a boom in the economy.

This car was used to transport the Ethniki Orgánosis Kipriakoú Agónos (EOKA) leader, General G. Grivas Dighenis. It is one of the few reminders of the guerrilla group.

ENOSIS

The end of World War II increased Greek Cypriot calls for enosis, or union with Greece. Fearing marginalization, the Turkish minority, which made

A UN observation point. Although hostilities along the "green line" do break out occasionally, the atmosphere has quieted considerably since the days of the partition.

up about 20 percent of the population, was hostile to this demand. Likewise, Turkey viewed the development of a potentially hostile state to its immediate south with some alarm. Britain was eager to hold on to Cyprus as part of the military presence of NATO (North Atlantic Treaty Organization) in the Middle East, and so discouraged enosis. In 1955 Greek guerrilla groups stepped up in actions against the British, who were increasingly viewed as an occupation force. The National Organization for Cypriot Struggle (*Ethniki Orgánosis Kipriakoú Agónos*, EOKA) bombed military buildings and attacked opponents of enosis, killing both British officers and Cypriots. Turkish Cypriots formed their own terror units, campaigning for *taksim* (tahk-SIHM), or division of the island. The British government drew up proposals for self-government, but the Greeks continued to pursue their nationalist aspirations. The two Cypriot communities became more polarized, and communal violence escalated into civil war in 1958.

Under pressure from the United States, the Greek and Turkish governments came to an agreement in 1959 that was accepted by the British government and leaders of the Greek and Turkish Cypriot communities. Cyprus became an independent republic on August 16, 1960. The agreement stated that Cyprus would not unite with any other state or be subject to partition. Britain agreed to guarantee the island's sovereignty and military security in exchange for maintaining two military bases on the island. To prevent minority discrimination, Turks and Greeks were represented separately in the parliament, administration, police, and army.

INDEPENDENCE

The first independent elections were held in 1960, resulting in Archbishop Makarios winning 30 out of the 35 Greek parliamentary seats, while

THE GREEN LINE

The "green line" (often referred to as the ceasefire line) was named after a British officer marked the dividing line between the Greek and Turkish sectors of Nicosia on a map in green ink in 1963. The term is used today to describe the UN-monitored divide that runs through Nicosia. UN troops have been in Cyprus since 1964 to ensure the safety of the minority Turkish enclaves following a breakdown in ethnic relations. After the Turkish invasion in 1974, the UN troops' task became much bigger, monitoring the 112-mile (180-km) "Attila" line that divides the Greek south from the Turkish north. The "Attila" line was named after the Turkish military operation that resulted in the invasion of North Cyprus in 1974. Turkish and Greek Cypriot troops face each other across this buffer zone, while the no-man's-land in between is garrisoned by UN forces from the UN Peacekeeping Force in Cyprus (UNFICYP).

Dr. Fazil Küçük and his supporters won all 15 Turkish-Cypriot seats. Makarios became Cyprus's first president, with Küçük as his deputy. In 1963 political disagreement arose, and fighting broke out between the two communities. Nicosia was divided—as it is today—by a ceasefire line, called the "green line." Turkish Cypriots were reduced to living in a few urban enclaves and became reliant on relief packages for food and other essentials.

The situation increased tensions between Turkey and Greece. By 1964 the United Nations had agreed to send a multinational peacekeeping force to replace British peacekeeping efforts. However, fighting intensified, and Turkish military aircraft intervened in some actions. Both Greece and Turkey began secretly sending regular troops to train and reinforce the warring factions.

In 1967 violence between Greek and Turkish Cypriots led to Turkish threats to invade. The Greek military junta of the time agreed to withdraw their regular troops, and an uneasy peace was established. Turkish Cypriots were allowed to leave their enclaves and live and work where they pleased. Makarios was reelected president in 1968 and again in 1973. The Greek junta's relations with Makarios worsened because he was thought to be

There are several villages inside the UN buffer zone that are home to some 10,000 people. The village of Pyla is famous for being the only village on Cyprus where Greeks and Turks live side-by-side.

content with Cypriot independence, while many Greek Cypriots still wanted union with the mainland. A struggle for power within the Greek nationalist community ensued. The current president of Cyrus is Dimitris Christofias, who was elected in the February 2008 elections.

PARTITION

On July 15, 1974, mainland Greek military officers who supported the nationalist cause led a violent coup against Makarios and his republican supporters. Many left-wingers and republicans were murdered, and the presidential palace was left in ruins. The long-awaited enosis had been achieved overnight. Most of the population, both Greek and Turkish, looked on helplessly, while Makarios escaped to the safety of the British military base at Akrotiri. Nikos Sampson, a right-wing radical, was proclaimed president. However, Turkey would not tolerate the establishment of an overtly nationalist government that would potentially threaten its southern coast. Five days after the coup, Turkish troops landed on the northern

Greek Cypriots made up 82 percent of the population in northern Cyprus before the Turkish invasion. Almost all of these people became refugees and moved to the south.

A soldier stands guard along the "green line."

Today there are around 3,000 British troops based at Akrotiri and Dhekelia, most of them working in electronic intelligence and surveillance for the British and U.S. military. In recent years the Cypriot government has demanded the return of the land and the closure of the base. In July 2001, locals protested at the bases, angry over British plans to construct radio masts as part of an upgrade of British military communication posts. They argued that this would damage the environment and increase the risk of cancer to local residents. The British have shown no intention of giving up the bases, although they have offered to surrender 45 square miles (117 square km) of farmland as part of a UN-brokered peace plan.

beaches of Cyprus, establishing a base around Kyrenia that linked to the Turkish sector of Nicosia. Vigorous fighting ensued.

Events in Greece created further confusion, with the fallen junta being replaced by a democratic government under Konstantinos Karamanlis on July 23. However, agreement was not reached among the guarantor powers, Greece, Britain, and Turkey until August 16, by which time the Turkish army controlled 37 percent of the island. As many as 165,000 Greeks fled the northern part of the island, leaving their possessions and property behind. Many lived in hastily erected camps in southern Cyprus for months. Around 51,000 Turkish Cypriots were thought to have fled to the north to escape the bloody reprisals of Greek nationalists.

In 1983 the Turkish part of the island declared itself an independent state, the Turkish Republic of Northern Cyprus (TRNC). However, except for its ally and sponsor Turkey, no countries in the world recognize its legal independence. UN-sponsored talks took place in 1992, 1995, and 1999 to try to come to a lasting settlement, but there was little real progress. A divided Cyprus joined the European Union (EU) in 2004, along with nine other new members from Central and Eastern Europe. The division of Cyprus has remained a source of conflict that has soured relations between Turkey and Greece, which are both members of the NATO alliance, and has also stalled Turkey's proposed membership in the EU.

GOVERNMENT

Turkish Cypriots at a political rally the day before the municipal and partial legislative elections in the Turkish Republic of Northern Cyprus.

CHAPTER 3

C YPRUS CURRENTLY HAS TWO governments. The Greek Cypriot-dominated Republic of Cyprus is still the legal government of Cyprus. The Turkish occupation of the northern portion of the island, however, undermines the republic's claims to be entirely representative. Only the Republic of Cyprus is recognized by the international community.

The constitution of 1960 provided that Cyprus be headed by a Greek president and a Turkish vice president, elected for five-year terms by all Cypriot citizens. An elected House of Representatives had 50 seats that were apportioned along ethnic lines—35 for Greek representatives, and 15 for Turkish Cypriot members. However, this constitution never inspired great confidence among Cypriots. Greek Cypriots sought closer relations with Greece, while Turkish Cypriots feared for their minority status. Attempts by Greek Cypriot politicians to change the constitution caused the ethnic schism that leaves Cyprus divided to this day.

Right: Barbed wire and a forbidden zone sign demarcating the Turkish military zone.

THE REPUBLIC OF CYPRUS

As the official government of the island, the Republic of Cyprus still enforces the constitution of 1960. However, since the withdrawal of Turkish Cypriot participation in government in 1964, the joint provisions in the constitution have been altered to ensure a noncommunal, single-representative government and administration. The president represents the republic at all official functions. A council of ministers holds executive power, controlling public services, monetary policy, foreign policy, and the drafting and passing of laws.

A man reading newspapers outside the headquarters of the UBP party in Nicosia.

The council is drawn from the House of Representatives. In 1985 the number of seats in the House expanded from 50 to 80, of which 56 are for Greek parties. The representatives are elected by proportional representation. Although 24 seats are reserved for Turkish parties, Turkish groups have not been represented since the beginning of the ethnic conflict.

Local government in the republic is at district, municipal, and village levels. The government appoints district officers, while local councils and municipal mayors are elected.

Three observer members representing the Maronite, Roman Catholic, and Armenian minorities also sit in the House of Representatives.

POLITICAL PARTIES The oldest established party in the Republic of Cyprus is the Communist AKEL, or Progressive Party of the Working People, founded in 1941. A pro-Soviet party, the AKEL achieved much success during the first 25 years of the republic, averaging 30 percent of the vote. Despite the breakup of the Soviet Union, the party remains powerful in Greek Cypriot politics. The AKEL campaigns for a demilitarized, nonaligned, and independent Cyprus. The republic's other powerful party, the DISY or Democratic Rally Party, seeks greater integration for Cyprus with Europe, especially through membership in the European Union. Other parties include the EDEK or Socialist Party of Cyprus, the DIKO or Democratic Party, the

EDE or United Democrats, and the recently formed European Party, known as Evroko.

In parliamentary elections held in 2001, the AKEL won the most seats with 34.7 percent of the vote, but failed to win a parliamentary majority. The Democratic Rally, party of then-president Glafkos Klerides, came in second. In the most recent elections in 2006, the Progressive Party of Working People again led the polls with 31.1 percent of the vote, followed by Democratic Rally with 30.3 percent of the vote. The Democratic Party came in third, with 17.9 percent. An even spread of support for the major parties ensures that coalition politics dominates, under the leadership of the president.

PRESIDENTIAL ELECTIONS in February 1998 resulted in victory for Glafkos Klerides. In the first round of voting, Klerides and his party, the DISY, won 40 percent of the vote, as did his closest rival, George Iacovou, an independent candidate backed by the EDEK and DIKO. A runoff between the two contenders resulted in a narrow 51 percent to 49 percent victory for Klerides. In presidential elections in 2003, Glafkos Klerides ran again. The election was dominated by the UN plan to reunite Cyprus in the run-up to EU membership. Klerides was largely in favor of the plan, while leading opposition candidate Tassos Papadopoulos, head of the Democratic Party, wanted major amendments before he would accept it. Papadopoulos narrowly won the election with 51 percent of the vote, with Klerides trailing with 38.8 percent. More recently Dimitris Christofias became the Republic of Cyprus's latest president in elections held in 2008. Leader of the Communist Party, he defeated right-wing candidate Ioannis Kasoulides, gaining 54 percent of the vote.

THE LAW

The legal codes of the republic are based on Roman law. The republic has a separate police force and legal administration. The government appoints the judges, but the judiciary is entirely independent of executive power. Courts exist at the supreme and district levels. District and assizes courts

Dimitris Christofias (b. 1946), the Republic of Cyprus's current president, has the singular honor of being Cyprus's first—and the European Union's first—Communist head of state. Involved in trade union politics since his teens, Christofias studied social science in Moscow from 1969 to 1974, earning a Ph.D. in history. He served as general secretary of EDON (Cyprus Socialist Youth), the youth wing of the Progressive Party of Working People (AKEL), from 1977 to 1987. He held various high-level positions within the AKEL until 1991, when he was elected a member of the House of Representatives. He was re-elected in subsequent parliamentary elections in 1996 and 2001. He also became a member of the National Council, a body that advises the president. Throughout his election campaign he pledged to restart talks with the Turkish north to find a solution to the long-lasting dispute. After being sworn in as president Christofias vowed that, "the solution of the Cyprus problem will be the top priority of my government."

Approximately 115,000 Turks from the mainland have settled in northern Cyprus since 1974.

deal with civil and criminal cases, while the supreme court is the final court of appeal for cases from district courts and adjudication in constitutional and administrative law.

THE TURKISH REPUBLIC OF NORTH CYPRUS

A provisional body, the Turkish Cypriot Federated State (1975—83), was established to govern Turkish Cyprus soon after the Turkish invasion.

Following a stalemate in negotiations, the Turkish Republic of North Cyprus (TRNC) was declared in 1983, and the people approved a new constitution in a referendum in 1985. However, only Turkey recognizes the self-proclaimed state, and no other countries have direct communication links or diplomatic relations with North Cyprus. The TRNC relies on Turkey for much of its international sea and air links and trade. It also ensures that Turkey is a powerful player in TRNC politics.

The TRNC is a secular republic governed by a unicameral Legislative Assembly of 50 deputies. These deputies are elected every five years. The country is run by a council of 10 ministers appointed from the Legislative Assembly by the president, on the advice of the prime minister.

The north held its first multiparty parliamentary elections in 1993, removing the long-ruling National Unity Party in favor of a coalition of the Democratic Party (DP) and Republican Turkish Party (CTP). In 1996 a new coalition was formed between the two main right-wing, nationalist parties, the National Unity Party (UBP) and the Democratic Party, which held power for the next eight years. In 2003 the CTP and DP formed a new government, with CTP leader Mehmet Ali Talat becoming the new prime minister. In 2005 CTP deputy leader Ferdi Sabit Soyer took over as prime minister after Talat's election as president.

Current leader of the Turkish Republic of Northern Cyprus, Mehmet Ali Talat.

In elections in April 2009, the anti-unification UBP won power in northern Cyprus, gaining 26 seats in the 50-seat parliament with 44 percent of the vote. Their leader, Derviş Eroğlu, became prime minister. Although the UBP is against unification with Greek-dominated southern Cyprus, it seeks a two-state solution, and wants talks to continue.

THE PRESIDENT Presidential elections take place every five years. A candidate has to win at least 50 percent of the votes—an absolute majority—

to secure an outright victory. Otherwise the candidates who receive the two highest number of votes go to second-round voting one week later and the winner becomes the president.

From 1975 to 2005 the president of the Turkish Republic of Northern Cyprus was Rauf Denktaş. A committed nationalist, he tried to gain international recognition for the TRNC. However, his approach proved to be major barrier to reconciliation with southern Cyprus, and tended to polarize opinion on both sides of the divided island. In 2005 Rauf Denktaş retired from the presidency. Mehmet Ali Talat, the sitting prime minister, won the presidential election, becoming the TRNC's second president.

NEGOTIATIONS

Discussions between Greek and Turkish Cypriots were an ongoing part of the Cypriot political scene even before independence. Since the Turkish invasion, negotiators from both sides of the ethnic divide have met on many occasions in the hope of finding a solution to their differences. UN mediators have produced a plan in which Cyprus becomes an independent republic—with two zones—a proposal that both sides have broadly accepted in principle.

Nevertheless, over the years, negotiations have faced some stumbling blocks. The distribution of power between the two communities remains unclear. The Greek Cypriots campaign for a powerful central authority, which they would probably control by virtue of their numbers. Turkish Cypriots seek greater power for local districts, which would give them more autonomy. The Greeks seek freedom of movement within the whole federation, so Greek Cypriots would be able to return to their homes and land in the north. Turkish Cypriots, however, reject this plan, fearing that they might quickly become a minority in their own sector. The Greek Cypriots demand the withdrawal of Turkish troops from the island. The Turkish Cypriots, on the other hand, want a Turkish military presence to ensure their security and political rights. The presidency is also a contentious point. Although both sides agree that there should be rotating Greek and Turkish presidents, this may prove difficult to carry out in practice.

A.E. Yalman, editor of the Turkish newspaper *Vatan*, wrote in 1960: "Greece and Turkey have a common destiny. They are condemned either to be good neighbors, close friends, faithful allies—or to commit suicide together."

REUNIFICATION, THE UN, AND THE EU

In the years running up to Cyprus joining the EU, UN-sponsored negotiations tried to bring the divided island together with a lasting settlement. The UN wanted to reunify Cyprus under a federal structure, with the two communities sharing power. In 2002 a peace plan was tabled, but the leaders of both sides failed to agree to the UN plan by the March 2003 deadline.

As EU membership approached, a revised UN reunification plan was put before both communities in a twin referendum, held in April 2004. Turkish Cypriots supported the plan by a 65 percent majority, despite opposition from their president, Rauf Denktaş. However, in southern Cyprus, Greek Cypriots firmly rejected the plan, with more than three-quarters voting against it, following a campaign against unification led by hardline president Tassos Papadopoulos. Because both sides needed to approve the plan, the island remained divided when Cyprus was officially admitted into the EU in May 2004. Although the whole of the island is considered legally part of the Republic of Cyprus, only southern Cyprus, which is under the direct control of the internationally recognized government, enjoys the benefits of EU membership.

Further talks were held between leaders of the two communities in 2006, and again in 2008, after the election of Dimitris Christofias as Cypriot president in February 2008. Christofias had very good relations with the new Turkish Cypriot president Mehmet Ali Talat (elected in 2005), and many Cypriots were optimistic that a power-sharing agreement could be reached. Travel restrictions were lifted and border crossings were opened in the divided capital of Nicosia. However, the talks stalled, and the victory of the anti-unification National Unity Party (UBP) in elections in northern Cyprus in April 2009 made a quick resolution less likely.

Turkey also wants the situation to be resolved: Turkey's plans to join the EU are linked to a peaceful outcome of the Cyprus question. After Turkish Cypriots supported the UN-backed plan for power sharing in the failed 2004 referendum, the EU pledged to introduce policies to end northern Cyprus's international isolation, and has began giving economic aid to the country.

ECONOMY

A carpenter in his shop in Nicosia.

I N RECENT DECADES THE REPUBLIC of Cyprus has become prosperous as its service-based economy thrived amid the boom in the world economy in the late 1990s and the early part of the new century. In the past 20 years the economy has shifted from agriculture to light manufacturing and services, such as tourism, transport, banking, and property development.

In 2008 the International Monetary Fund (IMF) ranked Cyprus among the 32 most advanced economies in the world. However, the Cypriot

A vineyard in the Troodos region.

Cargo containers awaiting transport on a commercial dock.

economy is very vulnerable to changes in economic conditions elsewhere—so if tourist arrivals from countries such as Britain and Germany fall because of a downturn in the economies of those two countries, Cyprus suffers too.

Trade is vital to the Cypriot economy, since the island has few natural resources—food, fuel, machinery, and raw materials are all imported. Cyprus joined the European Union in 2004, and in 2008 it adopted the Euro currency and became a part of the Euro zone of countries, meaning that Cyprus's financial policies are decided by the European Central Bank. Despite the economic downturn of 2008 to 2009, according to the IMF, Cyprus was the only country in the Euro area to record positive growth in the first quarter of 2009.

Economic development in the Turkish Cypriot north is much slower than in the south, with very little foreign investment and a much smaller service and tourist industry. Many people in the north are still employed in traditional jobs, either in farming or working in the government sector. Turkey has given northern Cyprus a lot of financial aid over the years to support its economy.

THE WEALTHY REPUBLIC

Following EU membership the Republic of Cyprus adopted the Euro as its currency on January 1, 2008, replacing the Cypriot pound, while the north began to use the new Turkish lira.

Between 1960 and 1974, before partition, Cyprus operated a successful, free-enterprise economy based on trade and agriculture that was the envy of its neighbors. Since 1974 the south has created an economic miracle. The economy of the Republic of Cyprus is dominated by the service sector—tourism, property development, and financial services—making up more than 78 percent of the country's gross domestic product (GDP). Tourism is one of the most important sectors of the economy, followed by financial services and real estate. The country's dependence on tourism means that economic conditions in the rest of Europe have a huge influence on the island's prosperity. Because it is dependent on foreign revenue, the economy is vulnerable to changes in the economies of Europe and the Middle East. Still, the standard of living in the republic is higher than that in any of its eastern Mediterranean neighbors, and over the last 20 years, the economy of the Greek south has remained healthy.

Cyprus's main trade partners are Greece, Great Britain, and Germany, and more than 50 percent of the island's business is with the EU. Exports of commodities, such as citrus fruit, potatoes, grapes, wine, cement, clothing, and pharmaceuticals, have grown. Cyprus imports most of its consumer goods, petroleum, food, and machinery from the United States and the European Union. The republic helps offset the trade deficit through its massive tourist earnings.

According to recent statistics, 376,800 people are employed in Cyprus, with 18,200 registered as unemployed, a rate of 4.6 percent. Young people between the ages of 15 and 24 are more likely to be unemployed. Full-time employees work roughly 40 hours a week, while part-time workers work 21.5 hours.

AGRICULTURE Small farms were the backbone of the Cypriot economy when the country gained independence in 1960. Large-scale irrigation projects meant that crops, especially fruit and vegetables, could be exported to Western Europe. Following the Turkish invasion of the north, agriculture became unevenly distributed on the divided island, with citrus fruits, cereal crops, and tobacco remaining in the Turkish zone but most of the grape crop and the valuable potato crop located in the south. In 1978, 23 percent of the working population in the south was employed in agriculture. However, since that time, the agricultural sector has shrunk, employing just 3.9 percent of the workforce in 2009 and providing less than 3 percent of national GDP (2008 estimate).

Strangely for an island, Cyprus has a small fishing industry and imports most of its fish and seafood. This is chiefly because of a shortage of plankton in the island's waters. Plankton are tiny organisms that fish feed on for nutrients. Small fishing boats go for sole, whitebait, and red mullet, while commercial vessels look for swordfish.

INDUSTRY, which includes manufacturing, mining, and construction, contributes 19.2 percent to the republic's total earnings each year and employs a fifth of the workforce. Natural resources are few, so industrial development is limited. The manufacturing industry produces piping and cement from asbestos and gypsum. Bricks, tiles, clothing, footwear, and wood and paper products are also made.

FINANCE AND BANKING make up a significant part of Cyprus's service sector. This includes offshore banking—as many as 50,000 offshore enterprises are registered in Cyprus, including insurance companies, real estate firms, and consulting firms. The Cypriot government, promoting the incentives of a favorable tax system and reliable infrastructure, has had considerable success in making Cyprus an ideal base for offshore

A copper mine in Skouriotissa.

businesses, especially those wishing to do business in the Middle East. Most offshore companies come from the Russia, the United Kingdom, and Germany.

TOURISM has been a major part of the economy of Cyprus since 1960. Following the Turkish invasion of northern Cyprus in 1974, many tourist hotels and important cultural attractions were occupied by Turkish forces. However, following partition, the tourist trade in the Greek-controlled south rapidly recovered, with many new tourist developments and luxury hotels springing up around Paphos in the west, Limassol in the south, and Larnarka and Ayia Napa in the east. Since the mid-1980s tourism has been the largest source of foreign income for the Republic of Cyprus, making up 12 percent of GDP in 2008.

Between 1997 and 2008, every year between 2 and 2.6 million people visited Cyprus. Income from tourism increased noticeably from 2002 through 2007 after Cyprus joined the EU. Tourist numbers remained steady in 2006 and 2007, with approximately 2.4 million tourist visits in both years, mostly vacationers from Northern and Western Europe. However, the world economic downturn hit the tourist industry in 2008 and 2009. In 2008 there was a small decrease in tourist arrivals on the previous year, with tourist earnings down by 3.5 percent. Figures at the beginning of 2009 showed tourist earnings to have dropped by as much as 12 percent and arrivals were down by 15 percent as a result of the global recession.

TURKISH REPUBLIC OF NORTH CYPRUS

The north's diplomatic isolation from the international community has forced the TRNC to rely heavily on Turkey for external trade and investment. The country's economy and infrastructure have been integrated into that of the mainland, and the Turkish currency, the Turkish lira, is legal tender in the north. To compensate for the economy's frailty, for years Turkey has provided aid to nearly every sector of the TRNC economy, including tourism, industry, and education.

The majority of vacationers to Cyprus come from Great Britain, with 1.2 million British tourists visiting the island in 2007.

The economy relies heavily on agriculture and government services, which together employ more than half the workforce. As in the south, the service sector makes up a massive 69 percent of the economy. Much of this is concentrated in state administration, and less is dedicated to tourism, financial services, and real estate development.

Trade is also a significant sector of the economy. The TRNC exports citrus fruit, potatoes, and textiles to the United Kingdom and Turkey, and imports food, minerals, chemicals, and machinery. Most imported goods come from Turkey (60 percent) and the United Kingdom. A low tariff barrier for Turkish goods and the superior development of the Turkish industry means that Turkish imports remain cheap and more competitive compared to local products. This, and the use of the Turkish lira, has led to high levels of inflation imported from the mainland. These factors have limited the growth of small-scale manufacturing in the TRNC.

AGRICULTURE contributes 8.6 percent to the north's wealth each year. It employs 14 percent of the working population and is an essential foreign currency earner for North Cyprus. Most of the island's crops are grown on the Mesaoria Plain, including olives, potatoes, wheat, barley, and tobacco. Guzelyurt, an area around Morphou, is the market garden of Cyprus, where oranges and other citrus fruit are grown in abundance. Fishing and growing tobacco are the main activities on the remote Karpas Peninsula. The main fishing ports are Bogaz and Kumyali. Animal farming primarily involves chickens, sheep, and goats.

INDUSTRY, including manufacturing and construction, contributes 22.5 percent to GDP. Most industrial output is absorbed by the domestic market. The growth of local industry has been hampered by difficulties in reaching

A young girl helps her parents separate olives from their leaves.

Aid from Turkey to the Turkish North has exceeded $400 million annually in recent years.

THE TOURIST DOLLAR

Tourism has been Cyprus's biggest and most important growth industry since the partition in 1983, with the southern part of the island now receiving more than two million visitors a year. Visitors, who come mainly from Britain, Germany, and Scandinavia, swamp Cyprus from May to October, outnumbering the local population. The beaches around Limassol, the resorts of Ayia Napa and Protaris at Cape Greco in the far southeastern corner, and the historical town of Paphos in the west offer numerous first-class hotels and tourist facilities for those seeking sun and sand.

Most of these resorts have been developed since the partition. Forest stations have been built to accommodate tourists in the Troodos Mountains, and numerous forest trails have been developed. The boom in the tourist industry has had positive consequences for the republic's construction industry, with the building of many hotels, apartments, and restaurants. Tourist centers such as Ayia Napa, for example, were insignificant rural villages some 30 years ago, but with the explosion of tourism, they have developed into a vast complex of hotels, restaurants, clubs, bars, and recreational facilities. The ancient sites of Curium, Citium, Amathus, Khirokitia, and Paphos are an added attraction. Although tourism has made the south rich, many people complain about the negative environmental and aesthetic effects of large numbers of square hotels and apartment blocks in overdeveloped areas such as Ayia Napa and the beaches east of Limassol.

international markets, an inability to attract new investment, and the competition of cheap imports from Turkey. Clothing, cartons, and processed food products, such as juices and animal feed, are the chief exports. Construction makes up 8 percent of the economy, partly a result of the expanding tourist industry.

ENERGY Power supply is one area in which the two communities of Cyprus have managed to cooperate. Since most of the island's water reserves lie in the north of Cyprus, the republic, in exchange for water, provides the TRNC with most of its electricity.

TOURISM North Cyprus has a far less developed tourist industry than the south, but it has grown in popularity because of its reputation for unspoiled natural beauty. In recent years as many as 400,000 tourists visit northern Cyprus annually. Of these only a fraction comes from Northern Europe. Most come from Turkey and the Arab world. Since the late 1970s North Cyprus has been advertised as a shopping destination for Turkish tourists. Most tourists still stay in hotels in and around the beaches of Kyrenia and Famagusta. However, the recent economic downturn has also badly hit the fledgling tourism industry in North Cyprus, with job losses and hotels closed throughout 2008 and 2009.

TRANSPORTATION

Northern and southern Cyprus are served by separate transportation systems, and there are no services linking the two parts of the island. The Republic of Cyprus has 9,090 miles (14,630 km) of road, while the TRNC

A power station in Kyrenia.

has 1,500 miles (2,414 km) of road. Modern, four-lane highways link Nicosia with Larnaca and Limassol, and Limassol to Paphos. However, a substantial part of the road system in the rural and mountainous areas is unpaved. An extensive bus service allows Cypriots in rural areas to travel to the main towns and cities. The roads in North Cyprus are less developed than those in the south and are far less busy. Cypriots drive on the left side of the road, a relic of British colonial administration. There is no functioning railroad.

The main international seaports in the south are Limassol and Larnaca, both constructed after the Turkish invasion. Limassol and Larnaca act as transshipment terminals for cargo going to and from the Eastern Mediterranean. Today Larnaca mainly functions as a berth for oil tankers. Dekeleia, Moni, and Vassiliko also have port facilities with specialized oil terminals.

Cyprus's merchant fleet has grown at a massive rate in the last 20 years, with more than 2,000 ships registered. The island's main port is Limassol, one of the leading cruise ports of the Mediterranean and the home port of several cruise operators.

In the north Famagusta and Kyrenia still operate sea traffic with the Turkish mainland. Until the Turkish invasion, Famagusta was the island's most important sea port, handling 80 percent of all sea traffic. Today Famagusta only serves the Turkish region. Vehicle ferries operate between Famagusta and Mersin in southern Turkey, and during the summer season, passenger and car ferries also run to Kyrenia.

The republic's main international airport is near Larnaca, with connections to most European and Middle Eastern destinations, as well as links to North America. A smaller but busy airport has also been built at Paphos, mainly to handle tourist flights from Europe. At the height of the tourist season, dozens of flights come into these airports everyday. Cyprus Airways is the national carrier, owned jointly by the government and local businesses. Turkish Cyprus's chief international link is Erkan, a small airport east of Nicosia. Only two air carriers fly scheduled flights to Erkan—Turkish Airlines and Cyprus Turkish Airlines. Chartered flights carrying tourists from Britain and other parts of Northern Europe fly to Erkan but have to touch down in Turkey first.

ENVIRONMENT

Hikers in Avakas Gorge in Akamas Nature Reserve in southern Cyprus.

Cyprus's
environment is
under pressure
due to the boom
of the tourist
industry, among
other reasons.

THE MOST PRESSING PROBLEM THAT affects the Cypriot people directly in their everyday lives is the water shortage, which has led to strict water controls in many parts of the island.

Although all Cypriots have access to safe water, many urban as well as rural dwellers have to live with water rationing. Reasons for the water crisis include the lack of natural water reservoirs on the island, sea water intrusion into Cyprus's largest aquifer and uneven seasonal rainfall levels. Seawater intrusion causes increased salination and happens when salt water from the sea is drawn in and contaminates freshwater aquifers. The purity of the water supply is also threatened by industrial pollutants, agricultural pesticides, and a lack of adequate sewage treatment.

To protect the coasts from further degradation, several coastal areas in Cyprus have been zoned to protect them from more damaging development, in accordance with the Foreshore Protection Law.

Rapid expansion in tourism and urbanization has threatened Cyprus's nature and wildlife. It has been estimated that about 2,000 species of mammals, birds and plants are now facing extinction in Cyprus. In order to prevent further loss, some species are now protected. Since 1994 strict conservation laws

Right: Tourists on Aiya Napa beach.

Kouris Dam, the largest of a network of 107 dams in Cyprus, has seen a drop in water levels.

have been implemented to control hunting, preserve forests, and maintain the general health of the environment.

Over the last decade Cyprus has experienced a terrible period of drought that has contributed to the water crisis. Fortunately the island does not suffer from any other major natural hazard except for some moderate earthquake activity.

WATER CRISIS

Cyprus has been undergoing its worst water shortage for many years. This shortage is a result of prolonged dry seasons and lower than average rainfall over several years. Cyprus has suffered an acute decline in rainfall for more than 30 years. Since 1972 rainfall has dropped 20 percent and runoff into reservoirs has dropped dramatically by 40 percent.

Experts believe that Cyprus's water crisis is mainly due to climate change and global warming. Global warming causes the temperature to rise, bringing about droughts and desertification. The lack of water means there is inadequate water for irrigation. It also affects the quality of the soil. Many areas in agriculture, including the widespread growing of Cyprus's symbolic citrus trees, are being threatened because of the water shortage.

Water has always been highly valued in Cyprus, as the people are accustomed to regular periods of drought due to the nation's location and climate. Cypriots are concerned about this severe water shortage because it impacts on everyday life as well as the economy, in particular agriculture and tourism. Since March 2008 Cyprus has cut the supply of water by 30 percent.

Cyprus has one of the world's highest concentrations of reservoirs, but today, its reservoirs stand only at around 10 percent full. In 2007 it was estimated that almost 180 million cubic feet (5.09 million cubic meters) of water would be required to satisfy demand in Cyprus. To demonstrate how demand for water exceeds supply and how much of a problem the situation has become, Cyprus's largest dam in Kouris holds about 3 million tons (2.72 million metric tonnes) of water and only stands at 2.5 percent full.

In an attempt to solve its water shortage problems, Cyprus has relied heavily on its desalinization plants, which take water from the sea and purify it, making it fit for human use. However, this solution is not ideal, because these desalination plants are

A sign warning people not to swim or fish in the waters. The walls of a sewage treatment plant collapsed, releasing over 1,100 tons (1,000 metric tonnes) of sewage into the sea in Kyrenia.

able to supply less than half the water the country needs. The practice of desalination is also environmentally unfriendly because it consumes large amounts of energy and causes pollution by emitting greenhouse gases into the air.

In the short term the government of Cyprus has imposed restrictions on water usage on the general public in an attempt to conserve water. The government also imports water from Greece. Cyprus has bought 10.5 million cubic yards (8 million cubic meters) of water from Greece, which is transported by huge tankers. If rainfall levels do not improve soon, the government plans to build more desalination plants in order to convert seawater into drinking water. Some experts say that unless Cyprus gets used to the low rainfall levels by adapting its methods of farming and managing its water supply more efficiently, it will continue to suffer from a water shortage.

In spite of the long drought, there are some signs that the situation may improve because rainfall levels increased dramatically in 2009. The Water Development Department reported that the rains have contributed 13 million cubic yards (10 million cubic meters) of water into the island's reservoirs during January 2009. This represents an increase of almost fourfold over the 3.4 million cubic yards (2.6 million cubic meters) meters in January 2008. In

Litter on the beach on the Akamas Peninsula.

fact the rains have been so plentiful that in one 24-hour period, 4.2 million cubic yards (3.2 million cubic meters) flowed into the island's dams, increasing their capacity from 30.7 million cubic yards (23.5 million cubic meters) to 34.9 million cubic yards (26.7 million cubic meters). The dam that made the most gain in water inflow was Paphos's Asprokremmos Dam with 1.74 million cubic yards (1.34 million cubic meters), followed by Arminou Dam with 697,138 cubic yards (533,000 cubic meters) and the Kouris Dam with 502,253 cubic yards (384,000 cubic meters). This sudden increase in rainfall may mean a relaxation of water restrictions, making everyday life more convenient for everyone living in and visiting Cyprus.

COASTAL DEGRADATION

Cyprus boasts a beautiful coastline with a total coast length of approximately 457 miles (735 km). Unfortunately the coastline of Cyprus, like the coasts of many other countries in the Mediterranean, is suffering from severe coastal degradation and erosion.

According to the Ministry of Communications and Works of Cyprus, some of the major causes of coastal degradation are man-made. These include rapid tourist development, almost 90 percent of which takes place in the coastal areas. Extensive beach quarrying; dam construction; sand mining; the building of coastal structures, such as breakwaters and groins; and urban development too close to the shoreline are some of the factors that may have triggered and accelerated coastal erosion.

Continued coastal erosion not only causes ecological and environmental problems. Its effects cause socioeconomic problems as well. For example, a coastal town with critical coastal erosion may start to lose tourists and visitors, thus hurting local jobs and businesses. Loss of extremely valuable land, including recreational and tourist beaches, and damages to urban infrastructure are important for the economy of coastal towns that rely heavily on tourism.

In 1993 a project called Coastal Zone Management for Cyprus was launched by the Public Works Department of Cyprus to find ways to stop the severe erosion and improve the quality of the beaches with minimum impact on the environment. At the end of the project in 1996 master plans were prepared to ensure that the protection and improvement programs continue to be monitored and implemented. Since the master plans have been in existence, several important parallel breakwaters have been built and illegal groynes—fixed structures extended from the sea wall or shore—have been removed in an attempt to stop the erosion. The three priority areas that were identified as needing urgent protection are the coastal regions along Paphos South, Limassol, and Larnaca.

In 2000 the Ministry of Communications and Works began to work in partnership with the University of Athens to protect and improve a further three coastal areas—Kato Pyrgos Tillirias, Crysochou Bay, and Zygi-Kiti.

LOSS OF WILDLIFE

Cyprus has a great deal of wildlife and a unique spectrum of flora and fauna. However, an EU report published in 2009 found that in Cyprus many natural habitats and numerous species of plant and animals are under threat. Both wildlife and the natural environment in Cyprus are not being adequately protected.

The report found that only 21 percent of the natural habitats in Cyprus that had been identified as priority habitats are in a healthy condition, and only 18 percent of the species that had been identified as needing conservation are in a satisfactory state. Habitats along the coast of Cyprus, including sand dunes and wetlands, have been found to be in an unfavorable state. In the animal world, certain mammals and snakes may be facing extinction.

Although Cyprus adopted the EU Habitat Directive six years ago, there continues to be an alarming lack of information and knowledge on the

The Mediterranean monk seal is one of the rarest marine animals today, with its world population estimated to be just 500. Most live in the Aegean Sea, although the seal has been sighted off the northern coast of Cyprus. The monk seals' habitat has been destroyed by tourist activity and development along the coasts of the Aegean, and their food supply threatened by declining fish stocks in the heavily fished eastern Mediterranean.

THE AKAMAS PENINSULA

The Akamas Peninsula situated at the westernmost tip of Cyprus is a paradise for nature lovers. This remote and unspoiled region is so special that a number of environmental organizations and projects have been working in the area with the objective of preserving this stunning wilderness for future generations to learn from and enjoy. In particular, these organizations aim to safeguard the area's biodiversity by overcoming existing and potential threats. Some of these threats include local landowners who want to develop their land for commercial purposes and British forces who use the area for military exercises.

The Akamas peninsular covers an area of approximately 42,000 acres (17,000 ha to 17,297 acres (7,000 ha) of which are designated as state forests. The Akamas is well known for its interesting and varied flora and fauna—it boasts 600 different plant species and more than 100 different types of birds, mammals, and reptiles as well as many rare butterflies.

It is also possible to find large areas of near-virgin habitats and vegetation. The coastline is still mostly pristine and is rich in marine life. Green turtles continue to nest on the beaches and there is the occasional sighting of the rare monk seal.

condition of its key species and habitats. The monitoring schemes to ensure accurate data is collated to help ensure these species are properly protected are inadequately maintained.

Some of the primary causes that threaten Cyprus's wildlife include rapid urbanization and overdevelopment, including the building of houses and roads. The growth of tourism has also contributed to the poor state of wildlife in Cyprus today. Other factors include unsatisfactory agricultural and forestry practices.

Although Cyprus has signed up to be part of various conservation projects such as Natura 2000 and the Birds and Habitats Directive, much work remains to be done by the government to make sure that policies are being correctly and efficiently implemented. Failure to safeguard the environment can mean a decline in food production and may eventually impact economic prosperity and the welfare of the population.

The geology of the area, which consists of many natural habitats, is environmentally important. The Akamas range of hills, its gorges and caves are essential for the survival of a wide range of wildlife, rare vegetation and plant communities. Species such as the endemic Cyprus white-toothed shrew, hedgehogs, hares, and foxes can be found here, including several species of bats including the fruit bat. Unique species of reptilian fauna such as the spiny-footed lizard and the green toad are rare species that can only be found in any significant numbers in Akamas.

More than 30 species of endemic plants grow on the Akamas peninsula. On the northern slopes can be found the Orchis punctulata and the Orchis laxiflora, two of Europe's rarest orchids. Out of all the orchid species that can be found in Cyprus, about 50 percent are located in Akamas. Many of the species and vegetation found in Akamas today have survived because they have not been exposed to the dangers of insecticides. For example, the freshwater crab that still survives here has become extinct from many parts of Cyprus as a result of the use of DDT and other insecticides during the campaign to eradicate malaria in the early 1900s.

Although sand dunes and wetlands are under great threat in other parts of Cyprus, they are still in existence in Akamas, mainly in the Lara area. This allows the rare and endangered plant and vegetation communities to continue to prosper, as well as the animals that rely on them. For instance, the ghost crab, an endangered species that has disappeared from other tourist beaches in Cyprus, is now a protected species.

On the west coast of Akamas, on the isolated beaches of Lara and Toxeftra, the green turtle and the loggerhead turtle, still lay their eggs and nest here. The rare green turtle, with a population of under 1,000 in Cyprus, is now facing the threat of extinction.

Even with its beautiful and important geology and wildlife, the Akamas Peninsula has come under threat from a variety of human activities and causes, including forest fires, excessive hunting, military exercises, and overgrazing. Protecting the diversity of wildlife in this area of tremendous ecological value is important not just for Cyprus but also for the entire Mediterranean region.

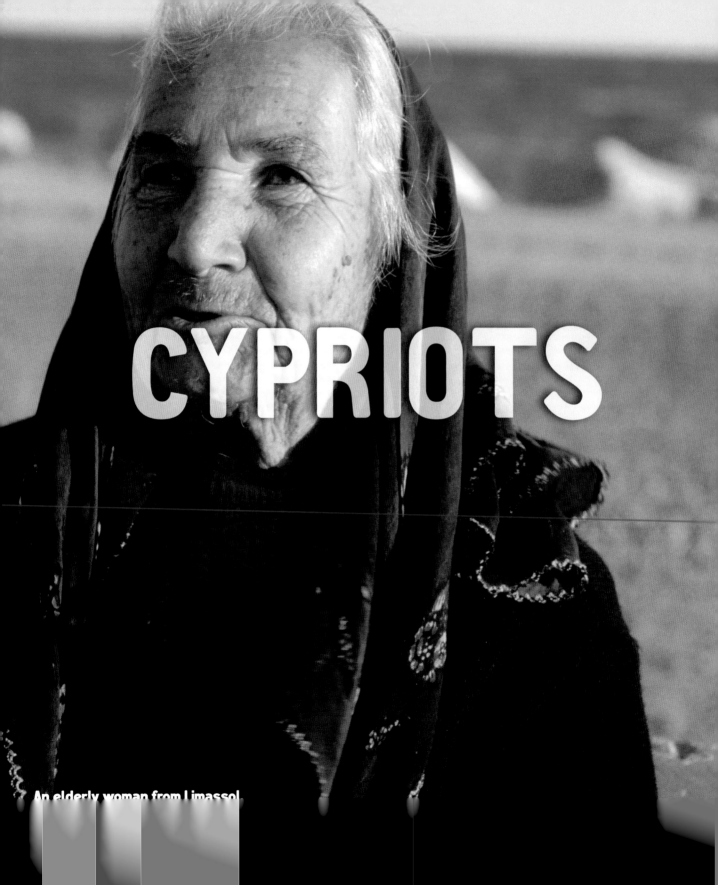

CYPRIOTS

An elderly woman from Limassol.

CHAPTER 6

THE OFFICIAL POPULATION OF Cyprus was 796,740 in 2009, although this does not take into account the large number of officially unrecognized Turkish settlers who have arrived since 1974.

Greek Cypriots make up 77 percent of the official population, Turkish Cypriots constitute 18 percent, while Maronites, Armenians, Greeks, and other Europeans contribute 5 percent. The Maronites, Armenians, and Greeks are classified as native Cypriots. The majority of around 80 percent of the population live in the prosperous Republic of Cyprus.

Both Greek and Turkish Cypriots immigrated in large numbers following independence in 1960 and again after the Turkish invasion in 1974. It is estimated that there are as many people of Cypriot descent living abroad as on the island itself. The majority went to the United Kingdom, and more than 100,000 Greek Cypriots live in London. Other English-speaking countries such as Australia, the United States, and Canada have also been popular destinations.

COMMUNAL STRENGTH, ETHNIC DIVISIONS

For many centuries, Cypriots lived in ethnically mixed villages, and by appearance it was impossible to tell the two communities apart. Nevertheless, despite 400 years of largely peaceful cohabitation, cultural and religious differences resulted in little genuine mixing between the two communities. Greek Cypriots remain culturally oriented toward Greece, speak Greek, and practice the Greek Orthodox religion, while

Most Cypriots define themselves in terms of their ethnic identity, and "Cypriot" is always prefixed with the qualification of either "Greek" or "Turkish." Both communities are proud of their heritage and customs.

Cypriots love to
gather in taverns
with friends.

Turkish Cypriots speak Turkish and practice the Islamic religion. Religious differences in particular have made intermarriage difficult and unlikely.

Since the partition of the island, the differences have become more pronounced, while the movement of refugees in both directions has meant that coexistence is virtually unheard of. Although history has created the schism in the Cypriot community, current attitudes further entrench the divide. Ethnic nationalism is rife—Turkish flags fly above many buildings in the north of the island, just as the Greek cross of Saint Andrew adorns every church and public building in the south. The Turks are clearly oriented toward the Turkish mainland, while the Greeks look toward Athens and Europe. Mutual mistrust and linguistic and cultural barriers continue to exist. Few Greek Cypriots now speak Turkish, and the only Turkish Cypriots who speak Greek are a few older people who worked for Greek businesses before 1974.

Although most Turkish and Greek Cypriots moved to their allotted sides of the Attila line following the division of the island in 1974, some small ethnic enclaves exist on both sides of the border. In the north only 250 Greek Cypriots, most of whom are elderly, still live around the village of Dipkarpas (known as Rizokarpaso by the Greek Cypriots) on the Karpas Peninsula, the remnants of some 20,000 Greeks who had lived there before the Turkish invasion. UN peacekeeping forces deliver food and mail from Greek Nicosia; relatives from Greek Cyprus are allowed to visit intermittently. Today Dipkarpas is also home to a large Kurdish minority. Surprisingly one biethnic village remains on the island, an example of how Cypriots lived before the partition. Situated where the Attila line buffer zone meets the British base at Dhekelia, the village of Pyla remains a vestige of the past, a perfect microcosm of the island before 1974. Greeks (67 percent) and Turks (33 percent) live in proximity but not always together, socializing in separate coffeehouses and attending separate communal schools.

GREEK CYPRIOTS

Through the centuries, Greek Cypriots have maintained their Greek identity. The retention of the Greek language and the establishment of the Greek Orthodox religion through the independent Church of Cyprus have become the twin bastions of the Greek Cypriot identity. The Greeks have clung fiercely to their roots because they were subject to constant invasion and conquest by foreign powers in the past. The Ottoman occupation, and more recently, the threat from Turkey have led the Greek Cypriot population to assert their identity even more firmly than they would if they did not feel threatened.

Almost all (99 percent) Greek Cypriots live in the south, and most have been abroad at some time or another. For those who can afford it, overseas education especially in Greece and Britain is popular. Most Greek Cypriots speak at least a bit of English. Because of this, Greek Cypriots think of themselves as Europeans, despite their geographical proximity and historical links to the Middle East.

Elderly men chatting in Paralimni in southern Cyprus.

TURKISH CYPRIOTS

Many Turkish Cypriots are descendants of the mainland Turks who remained on the island after the Ottoman conquest in the 16th century. During that period religion rather than ethnicity was the determining civic factor. Thus many of today's Turkish Cypriots do not trace their lineage to Turkey, but to a variety of sources, including the Balkans and Africa. Recent studies also suggest that some Turkish Cypriots are in fact descendants of Greek Cypriots who converted to Islam during the Ottoman period.

A Turkish Cypriot shepherd. The majority of Turkish Cypriots live in rural areas.

Since 1974 more mainland Turks have settled with their families in Cyprus to work on farms. These settlers are given TRNC citizenship if they remain on the island for more than five years. Turkish immigration has reinforced the Turkish identity of the north and created a stronger relationship with Turkey. However, social tensions have built up over the years. The Turkish Cypriots think that the mainlanders are increasingly controlling the economy and dictating the north's relations with the international community. They also believe that the steady influx of mainland Turks is slowly diluting the Turkish Cypriot identity, making them more Anatolian in character. In 2005 the TRNC tightened its control over Turkish immigration following an increase in crime and unemployment. This caused the first major disagreement between the TRNC and Turkey.

TRADITIONAL DRESS

Traditional dress is an important aspect of Cyprus's traditional culture, although today it is only worn on festive occasions. Cotton and silk, and a blend of the two called *itare* (IH-tahr-eh), are the main materials used. Silkworms are bred on the island and most materials are woven in the home. Traditionally the best festival dress is associated with marriage practices, especially dowry ceremonies. Items worn by the bridegroom, such as a silk handkerchief, are offered as a gift to his fiancée.

Compared to the dress of their mainland Greek compatriots, the clothes of Greek Cypriots are simpler and more uniform. For women two styles are most popular. The *karpasitiko* (karp-ahs-IHT-ih-koh) includes a white, long-sleeved dress with a high, round neck. Full white trousers, either plain or embroidered, are worn underneath the dress. A tight-fitting, long coat with decorated sleeves is worn over the top. The front of the coat is low-cut, to reveal the dress. On her head a woman wears an embroidered white or colored handkerchief, either draped or folded. Another popular choice is a black velvet, long-sleeved jacket worn over a long cotton shirt with a long, checked or striped skirt. A red fez or white handkerchief is worn on the head. Low-heeled, black shoes are worn with both types of clothing. Men's traditional dress includes a white, long-sleeved shirt and full, baggy black trousers tucked into black boots. A black sash is tied around the waist, and a black, embroidered vest is worn over the shirt. A small, black cap is worn on the back of the head.

For Turkish Cypriots, traditional dress derived from mainland Turkey is worn on festive occasions. Men will wear a red fez, and parts of the body are stained with red henna. Religion and custom decree that no hair should be seen, so both men and women wear a headdress. Until recently women covered their faces with veils or draped scarves. The basic dress has remained the same for many centuries—baggy trousers, called *shalvar* (shahl-VAHR), are worn by the women, along with a vest or a high-necked, calf-length jacket. Men also wear the *shalvar*, most often colored black or

Women wearing traditional dress in a parade.

blue. Short, embroidered vests, called *cepken* (chep-KEHN), are worn over high-necked, white shirts. Leather sandals with turned-up toes are worn by both men and women.

OTHER PEOPLES

Inevitably, because of the island's checkered and turbulent history, many other people have settled in Cyprus over the centuries. Although most have assimilated into the Greek or Turkish communities, a few groups, such as the Maronites and Armenians, retain a distinct identity.

MARONITES are an Arab people from Lebanon who practice a form of Catholicism. They first came to Cyprus with the Lusignan Crusaders in the 12th century, serving as archers against the Arabs. Saint Maron, a Syrian hermit of the late fourth century, and later Saint John Maron, the patriarch of Antioch from A.D. 657 to 707, are the founders of the Maronite religion.

Korucam (*Kormacit* in Turkish), north of Morphou, is the Cypriot Maronite capital, though only a few hundred Maronites still live in the village. They worship at a church in the village, Ayios Georgios, without interference from the Turkish authorities. Since the partition, most Maronites have moved to the south to seek a better life, and the community in Korucam is steadily declining. Maronites speak their native tongue, which is a dialect of Arabic mixed with many Greek and Turkish words.

Despite attempts by Muslim caliphs and the Ottoman Turks to subjugate and absorb the Maronites, today they constitute one of the major religious-ethnic groups in modern Lebanon.

ARMENIANS Trade links have existed with Armenia since ancient times. Armenians first arrived in Cyprus in the sixth century A.D., a consequence of struggles between the Byzantines and Arabs. When Armenia was brought under the influence of the Byzantine Empire, as many as 10,000 Armenians were forcibly settled in Cyprus by the Byzantine emperors to work the land. As fellow Christians, the Armenians had few problems assimilating into Greek Cypriot culture. However, with opportunities to immigrate to North America, Europe, and Australia, the Armenian community remains small in Cyprus, numbering just a few thousand today.

Cyprus has a notable expatriate population, mostly people from Northern Europe who have chosen to retire or set up a business there. Holiday homes and villas have been built in many parts of southern Cyprus to cater to the influx of people seeking to enjoy the island's dry, warm climate and relaxed atmosphere. The Cypriot government's favorable tax concessions and improvements in the infrastructure have helped this development. Cyprus's membership in the European Union in May 2004 also allowed nationals of any EU state the right to reside in Cyprus for up to three months. As many as 5,000 British nationals have settled there, mainly in the south around Limassol. Some own bars and restaurants around the popular tourist areas of Limassol, Ayia Napa, and Paphos, while some operate offshore businesses or are connected with the British military. Many of these people have come to Cyprus to retire in a country that retains strong economic and cultural links with Britain. Britain maintains military bases in Cyprus, where English is widely spoken. Many Germans and Scandinavians have also chosen to make Cyprus their home. There are also many Lebanese, Arab, Iranian, Russian, and Serbian entrepreneurs living in Limassol and Nicosia, usually running offshore banking and other services linked to interests in the Middle East and Eastern Europe.

The British military bases near Limassol and Larnaca give the two towns a very British feel at times, especially during the tourist season. The bases of Akrotiri and Dhekelia are miniature Britains, with pubs, housing developments, golf courses, and military hospitals to serve the military community. Most British soldiers are well behaved and are appreciated for the money that they spend in the bars, restaurants, and clubs on the island, but fights between soldiers and locals, and soldiers and tourists, occasionally occur. The conviction of three British servicemen for the rape of a Danish tour guide in 1996 caused distrust and resentment. Although such incidents are rare, it fuels tensions between the British military and the local population. In 1996 Cypriots held demonstrations against the British presence.

In the north foreign presence is far less noticeable. In the early and mid-20th century, the town of Kyrenia was a popular retirement place for former colonial officials. Before the Turkish invasion, some 2,000 expatriates, mainly British, lived in Kyrenia. By 1976 most had fled, and only 200 remained. With the establishment of peace and the growth of tourism, this number has increased in the last 10 years. Today Kyrenia remains a popular choice for British expatriates.

LIFESTYLE

Men spend a relaxing afternoon
together in a coffee shop.

FOR MANY CENTURIES, DESPITE the country's exposure to varied foreign influences, the traditional Cypriot lifestyle did not change much. The island's conquerors generally remained aloof from the Cypriot peasants, allowing them to get on with their lives. However, in the south, with increased prosperity and Westernization, lifestyle has changed dramatically during the past 40 years. This is a result of British influence and the south's gradual integration with the European economy.

More young Cypriots choose to leave their traditional villages and live in cities or even go abroad, where there are greater opportunities. Cyprus has a young population—68.5 percent of the people are between the ages of 15 and 64. These demographic changes have potentially far-reaching consequences for the Cypriot way of life. The attitudes and experiences of the young, which are very different from those of their elders, are increasingly dominant. Although the island has relatively low unemployment on both sides of the border, a lack of varied career opportunities still persuades many young Cypriots to leave.

The average life expectancy in Cyprus is 78 years (81 years for women and 76 years for men). The crime rate is extremely low on both

In spite of their ethnic problems, Cypriots' lifestyle remains relaxed. Cypriots are a laid-back people and this characteristic is evident even in the bustling cities of Nicosia and Famagusta, as well as in the towns and villages where the pace of life is slower.

sides of the divide. Major offenses, such as assault or murder, occur rarely, and theft is virtually unheard of.

VILLAGE LIFE

Before the Turkish invasion in 1974, there were more than 600 villages in Cyprus. The village was the core of Cypriot life for both Greeks and Turks. In bicommunal villages, Muslim minarets and church belltowers formed the same skyline. Today there are fewer and fewer inhabited villages where the traditional rural lifestyle remains. Despite this decline, village life remains important to many older Cypriots and is inextricably linked to notions of Cypriot identity.

The typical Cypriot village consists of a series of narrow roads and tracks linking outlying farms to the village. The village itself is centered around the village square. In the square there will probably be a church or mosque, depending on whether the village is Greek or Turkish; a coffeehouse; and

An old couple in the village of Kakopetria in the Troodos Mountains.

RURAL EXODUS

Since the 1960s there has been a very pronounced drift from village to town all over Cyprus, a trend accelerated by the ethnic conflicts and partition of the island. Cypriots are traditionally rural people. Before 1931 only 22 percent of Cypriots lived in a town, and until 1974, more than half the population lived in villages. Today in the south, approximately 70 percent of the people live in urban areas. The average age of the inhabitants in some of the more remote villages in the Troodos Mountains is 60 years, suggesting that many villages may become deserted in the near future. In the 1960s it was common for village residents to commute to the towns to work, since most villages were within an hour's travel to one of the six towns. However, a series of factors has led to a rapid expansion of the towns. They include the need for new housing created by the refugees who settled in Cyprus following the Turkish invasion, the increased modernization of life, especially in the south, the massive building boom, and the development of the coastal-based tourist industry.

Expectations for Cypriots have risen sharply. Apart from the influence of tourist development, the harsh village life has led many young Cypriots to look for better lives in the towns. Greater educational opportunities and a higher standard of living encouraged younger Cypriots to seek more than the simple rural life of earlier generations. The Paphos district, for example, had been a rural backwater offering few opportunities. During the 1960s and 1970s many Cypriots from the district migrated to other regions, since Paphos had limited work on the plantations along the coast. The Turks left after the 1974 invasion, further reducing the population by one-quarter, leaving many former Turkish villages deserted. Most of the young people work as hotel receptionists, bar staff, and cooks, suggesting that although the district is now prospering, vital, traditional links with the rural way of life are being lost.

The Cypriot government has introduced many plans to improve agricultural life and rural infrastructure, such as irrigation projects and building local schools, in an attempt to promote the village lifestyle and protect the rural heritage. In 2007 the Cyprus Tourism Organization launched a program called "Rural Tourism" to promote the attractions and culture of the countryside. The new inhabitants of many villages are often wealthy outsiders who have no particular link to the district. However, they are poor cultural substitutes for the communities that once existed.

Men at a coffeehouse. Coffeehouses are an integral part of Cyprus's society, where mostly men can come together and discuss local issues.

a number of stores. Men tend to begin work at dawn, often finishing their farm chores by midday. Irrigating the crops is an essential daily activity on this sun-parched island, and it is the difference between success and failure for the farmer. Stocks of water and underground reservoirs are constantly monitored. The coffee shop is the fulcrum of the village for the men, where news and gossip are exchanged. Traditionally women are excluded from this activity, and are usually found either looking after the family or working in the fields. Even old women will help bring in the harvest and tend the livestock. Nevertheless life is not just about work for Cypriot women. They often sit in shady backstreets to embroider, knit, and gossip. On the weekends villages burst into activity. The extended family gathers to eat and exchange news, and the taverns and coffee shops are at their liveliest. During festival times, processions, feasting, music, and dancing transform the village, bringing it to life.

HOSPITALITY

Hospitality is one of the cornerstones of the Cypriot way of life, and Cypriots are usually generous and gracious hosts. Even the poorest peasant feel bound to honor guests as lavishly as they can afford to. Turkish Cypriots are far less exposed to foreigners than their Greek counterparts, and consequently treat guests, or in Turkish, *misafir* (mihs-ah-FEER), with lavish cordiality and generosity. Typically Turkish Cypriots will ply their guests with food and drink, especially coffee.

HOUSING

The traditional rural dwellings of Cyprus have maintained the same character for many centuries. Most of them are functional because farmers

COFFEEHOUSES

The coffeehouse, or kahve *(kah-VEH) in Turkish, or* kapheneia *(gahf-EHN-ee-ah) in Greek, is a permanent and defining aspect of the life of the island, especially in the villages. Coffeehouses are mostly male-dominated establishments. Sitting in coffeehouses and discussing the issues of the world—whether those are money, soccer, weather, or politics—is the favorite pastime of most Cypriot men. Commonly located in the village square, the coffeehouse provides a public meeting place for the men of the community to discuss local issues, relax, and exchange gossip. Men will often spend many hours playing backgammon or card games. Increasingly coffee shops are also equipped with television, though the television is generally turned on only for soccer games or movies. Before the partition, most villages had two coffeehouses, one for the Turkish community and one for the Greek, but today this is no longer necessary.*

Hospitality is the hallmark of the coffeehouse, and strangers who hesitate at the door will generally be invited in. The coffeehouses are usually open all day, and often the men will gather there early in the morning before starting work for a quick cup of coffee. At the end of the day, they will also settle down at the coffeehouse for another cup . Coffeehouses sell mainly coffee and cold drinks, including beer and spirits. The coffee is normally very strong and drunk in small quantities, accompanied by a glass of water to wash it down. In the evening the men might switch to brandy. In small, isolated villages, the coffeehouse even serves as a local store and post office.

believe that dwellings should only be big enough to accommodate their inhabitants, while the surrounding land should stretch as far as the eye can see. The houses are built around a courtyard, with a beehive-shaped clay oven in the center.

In the towns of the south, modern dwellings are two-story, airy buildings built in a style found throughout the Mediterranean. The centers of Limassol and Larnaca are dominated by high-rise buildings, an increasingly familiar sight throughout Cyprus. Many wealthy Cypriots and expatriates build villas for themselves on the edge of the towns. The urban areas have rapidly expanded, swallowing many smaller villages in the process.

Traditional rural dwellings were constructed partly with stone plundered from ancient Greek and Roman dwellings, and from Venetian fortifications.

FAMILY AND MARRIAGE

The family has always been an important part of Cypriot society, for both the Greek community and the Turkish Cypriot community. When Cypriots speak of their families, they do not only mean their immediate relations; the family circle extends to second cousins and further. Families are a great source of support and pride, and kinship links are kept religiously. Family members are obliged to help one another at any time and in any way possible, including lending money, helping with employment or establishing business contacts, building homes, or finding suitable marriage partners.

Cypriot parents are willing to sacrifice a great deal for their children, and no expense is spared in ensuring that they attain a high level of education. Traditionally, marriages are arranged in Cyprus, and although this custom is still practiced, it is more common now for the young to choose their own partners. After marriage women are expected to look after the house and rear children,

For Greek Cypriot weddings, the church service is held on a Sunday, because any other day is considered unlucky.

and leisure activities are limited to watching television and visiting relatives. Although these restrictions are not as widespread in modern Cyprus as they have been in the past, much of this traditional morality lingers, and women have to be careful of their behavior.

Men, on the other hand, as the breadwinners and heads of the household, and they are allowed, and expected, to pursue their own entertainment and pleasure. Cyprus is still very much a male-dominated society, and women are characterized in conservative terms. Although women rarely venture into male-dominated professions, such as law and politics, many women today have paid jobs. Greater economic independence has helped free them from the restrictions of traditional, sex-designated roles. Although divorce

WEDDING EXPENSES: THE DOWRY

Traditionally fathers choose their daughters' marriage partners. In doing so, they bear responsibility for the future happiness of their children. This acceptance of responsibility is expressed through the giving of a dowry, or gift, to the daughter to accompany her in the marriage. The dowry is often substantial. It is traditional and desirable to provide a home for the newlyweds, which is also a useful method of passing on property from one generation to the next. The bigger the gift, the more favorable the girl's marriage prospects, since a generous dowry will attract wealthier and better suitors. Traditionally it is considered a disgrace for a daughter to remain unmarried, so fathers will build a house at almost any cost to avoid the shame; few suitors would be interested in a girl without property. Poorer families may have to stretch the construction over many years, while the rich will build property as early as possible. Preparing a dowry is an enormous expense to the parents, although this practice is in decline in modern Cyprus.

statistics are rising, marriage is still the life choice for the vast majority of young Cypriots. Since 2004, in line with EU laws, homosexuality has been made legal on both sides of the dividing line, and gay life does exist, but only in the tourist areas. Cyprus remains a socially conservative country where homosexuality is seen as immoral.

EDUCATION

The average educational career, from primary to tertiary education, is 14 years (13 years for males and 14 years for females). Cyprus spends 6.3 percent of its GDP on education. The literacy rate is 97.6 percent.

In the south one year of pre-primary education for 3-year-old children has recently been made compulsory. Elementary education is mandatory and free for all children from age 5 to 12. Free secondary education lasts for another six years. This includes three years at a gymnasium or a preparatory college and three years in high school. There are three state universities as well as many private universities. The state universities are the University

The Greek Cypriot wedding ceremony retains many traditional features. If it is a village wedding, the whole community will be invited to attend. If it is in a town, an announcement inviting guests to the wedding is placed in the local newspaper.

A school choir performance. A well-rounded education, which includes learning music, is important to all Cypriots.

of Cyprus that opened in 1992, the Cyprus University of Technology, and the Open University of Cyprus. An education overseas is still the choice of many Cypriots, with up to 10,000 going abroad each year, especially to Britain and Greece.

In the Turkish north, education is free and compulsory for all children from age 7 to 15. Further education is provided for 16- to 18-year-olds at high schools. Higher education is state-provided. Universities include the Eastern Mediterranean University near Famagusta and the Cyprus International University.

WORK AND WELFARE

Working hours throughout the island revolve around the Mediterranean siesta. Typically shops are open from 8:00 A.M. to 1:00 P.M. and 2:30 P.M. to

5:30 P.M. in the winter, and from 7:30 A.M. to 1:00 P.M. and 4:00 P.M. to 7:00 P.M. in the summer. The Cypriot government operates a comprehensive social insurance program that covers all working adults and their dependents. Benefits from the program cover unemployment, sickness, maternity leave, injury at work, and old-age pension. All contributions to the program are income-related. Workers are protected against unjust dismissal. Unemployment is low in the Greek portion of Cyprus, standing at approximately 3.9 percent.

In the north, although official statistics suggest an extremely low rate of unemployment, there is considerable underemployment, particularly in farming. Most people work, but do not have quite enough to be prosperous. As a result of regular high inflation, a minimum wage is fixed by law for all occupations and determined by a commission including the government and employers. A cost-of-living allowance is also paid to offset the effects of high inflation. However, although government bodies pay the allowance regularly, private companies do not. This has led to public sector employees becoming wealthier than their private sector counterparts. With the opening of the borders in 2003, it is estimated that thousands of Turkish workers travel to work in the south each day through the British base in Dhekelia. Although some work on the base, many travel farther to work on building sites in the south. Others work in temporary or seasonal jobs as waiters or cleaners. A large number of Turkish Cypriots also use the airport in Larnaca to fly to other European cities to seek work.

A Turkish Cypriot artisan at work.

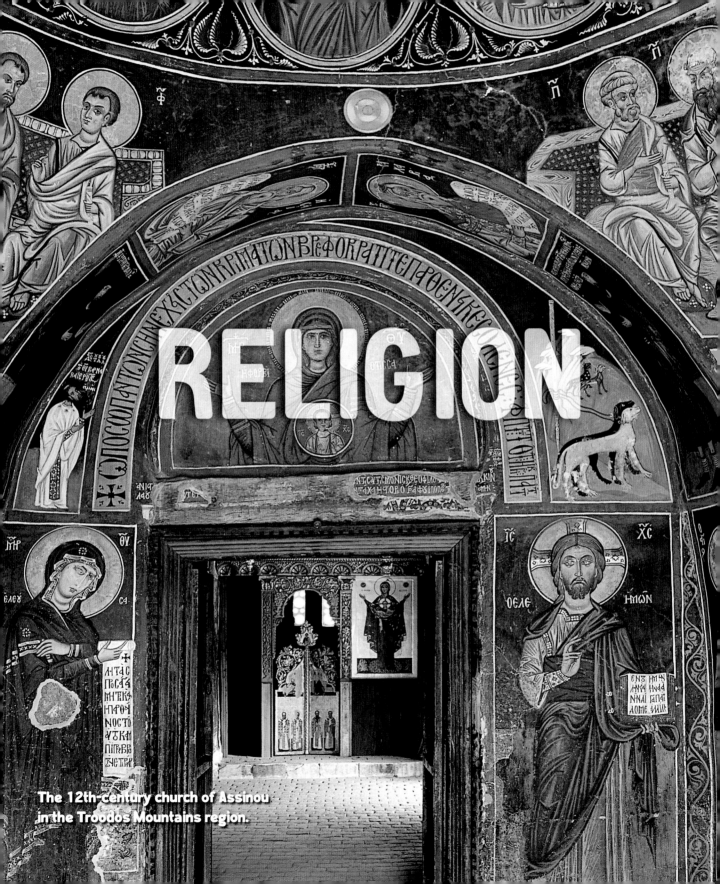

RELIGION

The 12th-century church of Assinou
in the Troodos Mountains region.

R ELIGION IN CYPRUS REFLECTS both the island's complicated history and its ethnic composition. There are Muslim mosques, Orthodox churches, Armenian churches, and Catholic cathedrals, an indication of the many faiths that have found adherents in Cyprus over the years.

There are two main religions in Cyprus. The vast majority of Greek Cypriots follow the Orthodox faith, while Turkish Cypriots practice Islam.

Seventy-eight percent of the population is Greek Orthodox, 18 percent is Muslim, and the remaining 4 percent practice other religions such as the Maronite and Armenian Apostolic faiths. In North Cyprus 98 percent of the people are Muslims, and the remainder are Maronites, Orthodox Greek Cypriots, and followers of the Armenian Apostolic faith. Despite a wide belief in religion, observers have noted a decline in religious observance. Islam is not practiced with great fervor, and some Cypriot Muslims have a relaxed attitude toward mosque attendance.

The partition of the island has segregated Cyprus into an Islamic north and an Orthodox south. Only a few churches remain open in North Cyprus, including Ayios—the Greek word for "saint"—Mamas near Morphou, and Saint Andrew's Church in Kyrenia. Many other churches in the north have either been converted to mosques or museums, or desecrated by the Turkish army. South of the partition line, a mosque still operates in each of the cities of Larnaca, Limassol, and Nicosia to serve the needs of the republic's large population of Arabs, Iranians, and the remaining Turkish Cypriots. The other mosques, left empty since the Muslim migration to the north, are locked and maintained by the government.

THE CHURCH OF CYPRUS

The huge number of Orthodox churches throughout the island and the beauty of the frescoes and icons inside them bear testimony to the island's strong Orthodox Christian traditions. The majority of Cyprus's Greeks are Orthodox Christians, a part of the Eastern Orthodox faith that is dominant in Greece, Russia, and much of Eastern Europe. However, Cypriots have their own independent church, the Orthodox Church of Cyprus. Although similar in practice to the Greek Orthodox Church, the Church of Cyprus is not under the authority of an external patriarch. In A.D. 488 the Byzantine emperor Zeno granted this privilege to Archbishop Anthemius. Since the 18th century the Cypriot clergy has played a prominent social and political role on the island, mainly as a result of the Ottoman style of rule that gave both secular and religious authority to the clergy. Consequently the archbishop of Cyprus was also given the title of "ethnarch," or national leader of the Greek community. The archbishop is elected by representatives of the towns and villages of Cyprus.

The Church of Cyprus is estimated to have more than 700,000 members, divided among six dioceses across the island.

The church and monastery of Saint Barnabas.

SAINT PAUL AND SAINT BARNABAS

It is mentioned in Acts 13 of the Bible that Cyprus was Saint Paul's first missionary destination. Born in Tarsus, under the name Saul, Saint Paul, together with the apostle Barnabas, set sail to Cyprus from Seleucia. It was after his departure from Cyprus that he changed his name to Paul. In Cyprus, Paul and Barnabas first went to Salamis then traveled throughout the entire island preaching and proclaiming the word of God in synagogues. When they reached Paphos, they met the magician Elymas, also known as Bar-Jesus, who was a Jewish false prophet. The magician opposed them when they attempted to preach the word of God to the Roman proconsul, Sergius Paulos. However, Paul rebuked Elymas and blinded him temporarily, thus allowing them to successfully convert Sergius Paulos to Christianity. However, according to the Bible, before Paul was able to make the Sergius Paulos believe in the teachings of Christianity, the local pagans lashed him to a marble pillar and "scourged him 39 times." This pillar is now known as Saint Paul's Pillar, which is now a famous tourist attraction in Paphos.

One of the island's most famous monasteries is named after Saint Barnabas, companion of Saint Paul, and one of those responsible for bringing Christianity to Cyprus. Barnabas was born in Salamis and is revered as the founder of the Cypriot church. He was martyred by stoning in A.D. 75, having angered the Salamis Jewish community.

The discovery of Barnabas's bones buried beneath a carob tree on the Mesaoria Plain in the late fifth century provides the Church of Cyprus a foundation on which to claim its ecclesiastical independence. After the apostle's remains were unearthed, the archbishop of Cyprus went to Constantinople to ask for the Cypriot church to be granted autonomous status. The Byzantine emperor Zeno agreed, persuaded by the gift of the original copy of the Gospel of Saint Matthew, supposedly handwritten by Barnabas and found clasped in the dead saint's arms. The tomb of Barnabas is at the Monastery of Apostolos Varnavas (Barnabas), situated north of Famagusta. Cypriots of all faiths still revere the location.

Orthodox worship is highly visual, and ritual plays an important role. Orthodox churches are richly decorated with religious art, including icons, frescoes, murals, and ecclesiastical vessels. The intention is to provide strong visual encouragement for the worshipers, stimulating faith and piety. Icons are positioned around the inside of most churches, and walls

THE MONASTIC LIFE

Monasticism is a long-established and essential feature of the Orthodox tradition, growing out the Roman emperor Constantine's unification of state and church. Cypriots are proud of their monastic traditions and institutions, especially the magnificent hilltop monasteries of Panagia tou Kykkou, Machairas, and Stavrovouni. The monasteries have borne the ideals of Orthodox Christendom through time despite numerous foreign invasions and occupations. Cyprus contributes more monks to the monastic enclave of Mount Athos, the most important center of Orthodoxy in northern Greece, than any other Orthodox country.

Although their numbers are falling, people still join monasteries. The Stavrovouni Monastery, near Larnaca, is considered the strictest one on Cyprus. There 20 or so monks maintain the traditional monastic lifestyle. Most of the monks are young and have to be highly committed to a life that makes great demands on them. Their day is divided equally between prayer and study, physical labor, and rest. During the rest periods, the monks eat two frugal meals without meat and carry out nightly prayers that constantly interrupt their sleep. The main liturgies (prayers) of the day are practiced in the courtyard. They include predawn "matins," the main liturgy after sunrise, "vespers" before the evening meal, and "compline" later in the evening. Winters in the monastery are very severe, making the monks' farming activities difficult. The monks still paint icons, which are of a very high standard, while many monasteries produce their own wine and make their own jam and honey.

Other monasteries, such as Ayios Neophytos near Paphos, are popular places of pilgrimage. Ayios Neophytos was established by Neophytos, a local saint, in the 12th century. Neophytos, who had come to the hills of Paphos to seek solitude, cut a hermitage into the rocks with his own hands. Soon a sizeable community sprang up around the famous monk, who was revered for his holiness and wisdom. He was a scholar of considerable note, and his handbook on monastic life, Ritual Ordinance, *survives to this day. Today pilgrims come to see the bones of the monk in the cave hermitage and to view the beautiful religious frescoes painted by followers of Neophytos.*

are covered with frescoes depicting religious events and symbolizing religious ideas. An iconostasis—a highly decorated partition that divides the sanctuary from the rest of the church—is also a part of Orthodox worship. The congregation looks into the sanctuary through doorways in the iconostasis. On each side of the doorways are icons representing Jesus Christ, the Virgin Mary, the Four Evangelists, and the Last Supper. Symbolically the iconostasis represents a religious presence during services, a filter through which the faithful may worship. Orthodox believers always pray standing, light candles as offerings, and often kiss the icons as a sign of respect and supplication. The combined experience is intended to convey the mysterious essence of the faith. The priest will wear garments that have symbolic meaning.

The Lala Mustafa Pasha Mosque in Famagusta in northern Cyprus.

ISLAM

Cyprus's Turkish minority is almost exclusively made up of Sunni Muslims. Authority for the Muslim religion in Cyprus is the mufti, an expert in Islamic law, and the Koran, the Muslim holy book. Generally the Muslims in Cyprus are not as devout as their mainland counterparts. Islam has never been politically or socially dominant on the island. This can partly be explained by the mixed background of the island's Muslim community, who had intermarried with both Lusignan and Venetian Christians. In the Ottoman period, a sect called Linovamvaki practiced Islam outwardly but maintained Christian beliefs in private.

ISLAMIC SECTS

A number of high-profile Islamic sects have prospered in North Cyprus recently. The best known is led by the charismatic Mehmet Nazim Adil, who leads the Naqshbandi-Haqqani order of Sufism. His home and the headquarters of his organization—the Turkish Cypriot Islamic Society—are in Lefke, near Morphou Bay. There are also groups abroad, including London. The society campaigns for greater piety in the lax religious atmosphere of the north and stresses the authority of the spiritual leader.

In 2001 Mehmet Nazim Adil toured a number of Muslim countries, including Uzbekistan, parts of Southeast Asia, Pakistan, and Sri Lanka. He has also given talks all over the world, including the United States, Canada, and parts of Europe. Some well-known local and international figures have been followers. Actor Rauf Denktas, the British singer Cat Stevens (whose father is Greek-Cypriot), and the British rock musician Bob Geldof are more recent supporters.

Other sects included the 13th-century Mevlevi Order, which stressed music and dance as a way of expressing love for God. It lasted until 1954. The Ba'hai sect from Iran has also had substantial support, particularly in northern Cyprus. Given these unconventional influences, it is not surprising that Turkish Cypriots are not particularly orthodox Muslims. The more obvious expressions of Islamic devotion, such as wearing religious dress and growing long beards, are not popular with Turkish Cypriots. Islamic law, or shari'ah, is not practiced in North Cyprus or in Turkey.

Islamic principles differ slightly from those of Christians. Although Muslims believe that the Bible is a sacred book and recognize the teaching of the biblical prophets, they do not believe Jesus is divine; instead they believe he is merely a prophet. Muslims consider Muhammad the greatest and final prophet, the carrier of God's message to humankind. However, they do not worship Muhammad, only God, and God's revelations to Muhammad are contained in the Koran. Before beginning prayer, Muslims first wash their hands, arms, feet, ankles, head, and neck in running water. If water is not available, the ritual motions will suffice. They must then cover their head, face Mecca, and perform a precise series of genuflections.

OTHER FAITHS

Maronite Christians come from Lebanon, where the Maronite church is one of the largest eastern branches of the Roman Catholic Church. There are about 10,000 Maronite worshippers in Cyprus today. Most of them live in the south of Cyprus and have in part assimilated into the Greek Cypriot community. The church traces its origins to Saint Maron, a fourth-century Syrian hermit. The immediate spiritual leader of the Maronite church, after the Pope, is the patriarch of Antioch, who lives in Bkirki, near Beirut. The patriarch of Antioch remains head of the Catholic churches in the Middle East. Despite attempts by the Pope to standardize their rites into Latin in accordance with the rest of the Catholic world, the church retains the ancient West Syrian liturgy, although the vernacular language of the Maronites is Arabic. For some years the Maronites have celebrated Easter at the same time as the island's Orthodox community, in part because it is convenient.

There are also a few thousand practicing Roman Catholics in Cyprus. Catholicism has a long history on the island. Under Lusignan rule Catholicism was the religion of the local aristocracy. Many of the island's great religious buildings date from this time. They include the Saint Sophia Cathedral in Nicosia, the Saint Nicholas Cathedral in Famagusta, and the Abbey of Bellapais near Kyrenia. All of these buildings have since been converted to mosques or Orthodox institutions.

There are approximately 3,000 Armenians in Cyprus who practice the Armenian Apostolic faith. The Armenian Apostolic Church was founded in the late third century by Gregory the Illuminator, its patron saint and official head. In converting the Armenian king, Gregory in effect created the world's first truly Christian state. The Armenian Church separated from the other Eastern churches in the sixth century and is completely autonomous. It is headed by the Catholicos of Echmiadzin, near Yerevan, in Armenia. Catholicos is the title given to the head of the Armenian Church, and Echmiadzin was the former capital of the Kingdom of Armenia between the second and fourth centuries.

Anglicans in Cyprus also number a few thousand. They are sustained by the island's small British population.

LANGUAGE

A man reading a Turkish-Cypriot newspaper.

CHAPTER 9

BOTH THE GREEK AND TURKISH spoken on Cyprus are distinct dialects and differ from the languages of Greece and Turkey. It is estimated that about 15 percent of the words in the two local languages are peculiar to Cyprus. Curiously, to the untrained ear, Cypriot Greek and Turkish sound almost identical because of the strong intonation and accent.

In the republic, English is also widely spoken. This is partly a result of the British colonial past, but mainly it is because of the longtime presence of British military bases and the huge numbers of English-speaking tourists who visit the island each year. Speaking English is still seen as a badge of sophistication and education among Cypriots, both Greeks and Turks.

GREEK

Greek is an Indo-European language that can be traced back to the 14th century B.C., making it one of the oldest languages in the world. Many of the writing systems used today are based on ancient Greek. In ancient times Greek was widely spoken throughout the eastern Mediterranean.

Although the majority of the Greek Cypriot population spoke Greek, a local dialect has developed over many centuries. To some mainlanders the dialect seems to be a completely different language. Certain sounds

Posters in the Greek language.

in standard Greek are almost completely absent from Cypriot Greek, while in some regional dialects, such as in Paphos, the spoken language has been heavily influenced by Turkish words.

Greek is not an easy language to learn. The positioning of stress is an important part of speaking Greek, and emphasizing the correct syllable is essential for clear communication. An incorrect stress will render words unintelligible, or possibly change their meaning altogether. For example, the word *yéros* (YEH-ros), with a stress on the "e," means "old man," while the same sounds with a stress on the "o," as in *yerós* (yeh-ROS), means "sturdy." Greek has a number of longer vowel sounds, where two vowels appear side-by-side. The two vowels are usually read together as a single sound. However, if an accent is placed above the first vowel, the two sounds are pronounced separately, and the first vowel sound is given emphasis. Despite these difficulties Greek is a very beautiful spoken language.

In conversation Greek speakers differentiate between informal and formal address, and young people, older people, and rural folk almost always use informal forms, even with strangers. There are numerous words and phrases that are constantly used in Greek. The most common greeting is *yá sou* (YA soo), meaning "health to you," while *ti néa* (tee NEH-ah), meaning "what's new," is also used. If a Greek Cypriot wishes to express dismay, he or she will say *pó-pó-pó* (POH-poh-poh); *ópa* (OH-pah) means "watch it" or "whoops;" and if Greek speakers want you to slow down and relax; they will say *sigá sigá* (see-GAH see-GAH).

TURKISH

The Turkish language is a member of the Turkic family of languages, spoken by more than 150 million people living from the borders of China

The Greek alphabet used today was formed as far back as the Hellenistic period (300—100 B.C.), and has heavily influenced the formation of other alphabets, including the Roman alphabet. There are 24 letters in the Greek alphabet, and 13 main combinations or diphthongs.

A,a	a	"a" as father	O,o	o	"o" as in toad
B,b	v	"v" as in vet	P,p	p	"p" as in put
G,g	y	"y" as in yes			(sometimes like a "b" sound)
D,d	dh	"the" as in then	R,r	r	"r" as in terror
E,e	e	"e" as in wet	S,s	s	"s" as in sat
Z,z	z	"z" as in zebra	T,t	t	"t" as in tight
H,h	i	"i" as in ski			(sometimes like a "d" sound)
U,u	th	"th" as in theme	Y,y	i or y	"i" as in ski
I,i	i	"i" as in ski	F,f	f	"f" as in fish
K,k	k	"g" as in get	X,x	kh	"ch" as in loch
L,l	l	"l" as in lolly	C,c	ps	"ps" as in lips
M,m	m	"m" as in man	V,v	o	"o" as in toad
N,n	n	"n" as in no			
J,j	ks	combination of "k" and "s," not found in English			

to the Balkans in southeastern Europe. Modern Turkish is a descendant of Ottoman Turkish, which itself descends from Old Anatolian. Over the centuries Turkish has absorbed a great many Persian and Arabic words.

The Cypriot Turkish dialect is quite distinct from Standard Turkish used on the mainland. Turkish Cypriot usage is also very casual. Turks from Istanbul, for example, consider Cypriot Turkish a slovenly dialect, while the Turkish Cypriots view standard Turkish politeness and formality with amusement. Regional dialects also exist. Paphiot Turkish, spoken by Turkish Cypriot refugees from the Paphos district, shows the effects of a long cohabitation with Greek, containing many Greek words or variations of Greek words. However, the influx of mainland Turks and two decades of Turkish army occupation means that mainland Turkish is becoming increasingly influential. Some peculiarities of the dialect are steadily being eroded. The influence of Turkish television has also contributed to the harmonizing of the two languages. Sadly the Cypriot Turkish dialect could disappear over the next two generations, as the north slowly becomes absorbed by the mainland.

Turkish is notoriously difficult for Western European language speakers to learn, as the grammatical structure is unrelated to any Romance or Indo-European languages, and the word order is difficult. Turkish is characterized by a tendency to expand from an unchanging root word to which one or more of a vast array of suffixes or word endings are attached to change its meaning. For example: *bilgi* (bihl-GEE) means "knowledge," while *bilgisiz* (bihl-gee-SIHZ) means "without knowledge," and *bilgisizlik* (bihl-gee-sihz-LIHK) means "lack of knowledge."

However, Turkish pronunciation is easier than Greek because the spelling is phonetic, and words are pronounced as they are spelled. Turkish vowels are usually short, and unlike Greek, there are no diphthongs, or vowel combinations—each vowel retains its individual sound. Stress is generally placed on the last syllable of a word, with the exception of place names. Typical Turkish greetings include "*Nasilsiniz*" (nah-sihl-sih-NIHZ) and "*Ne haber*" (neh hah-BER), both meaning "How are you?" while typical phrases include "*bir dakika*" (bih dah-kih-KAH), or "wait a minute," and "*affedersiniz*" (ahf-ehd-ehr-sih-NIHZ), meaning "sorry" or "I beg your pardon."

NEWSPAPERS

The first Cypriot newspaper, published in both Greek and English, was circulated on August 29, 1878, under the name *Kypros* (*Cyprus*). The first Turkish Cypriot newspaper was circulated on July 11, 1889, under the name *Sadet* (*Hope*). Today Cyprus has a relatively developed press with a large number of dailies, weeklies, and periodicals reflecting a wide range of ideologies and covering a variety of subjects. Cypriots are a highly literate,

The Greek Cypriot dialect is said to have undeniable Homeric origins, supporting the widely held belief that the island's Greek inhabitants are descendants of Mycenean Greeks from the Trojan Wars.

Until 1928 Turkish was written in the Arabic alphabet. Since the Arabic alphabet was deemed unsuitable for representing the sounds of Turkish, the language underwent radical reforms, with Arabic letters being replaced by the Latin alphabet. Today the Turkish alphabet has 29 letters—eight vowels and 21 consonants.

a	"a" as in man	l	"l" as in land
b	"b" as in bet	m	"m" as in mud
c	"j" as in jam	n	"n" as in not
ç	"ch" as in church	o	"o" as in hot
d	"d" as in dad	ö	"er" as in other
e	"e" as in bed	p	"p" as in pot
f	"f" as in fat	r	"r" as in ribbon
g	"g" as in goat	s	"s" as in sing
ğ	"y" as in yet	x	"sh" as shall
h	"h" as in house	t	"t" as in take
ı	"i" as in cousin	u	"u" as in push
i	"i" as in pit	ü	"ew" as in yew
j	"s" as in treasure	v	"v" as in vast
k	"k" as in key	y	"y" as in yet
		z	"z" as in zebra

news-hungry people, as reflected in the many publications available on the island. This is partly a product of political organizations, such as trade unions and political parties, sponsoring publications on both sides of the divide. In the republic, popular daily papers in Greek include *Alithia* (*Truth*), a right-wing paper that supports the DISY party, and the moderate papers *Apogevmatini* (*Afternoon*). *O Phileleftheros* (*The Liberal*) is the oldest newspaper in Cyprus, with a large circulation of 26,000. *Ergatiki Phoni* (*Workers' Voice*) and *Ergatiko Vima* (*Workers' Tribune*) are popular weekly

Newspapers on sale at a newsstand.

trade union papers. *Haravgi* (*Dawn*) is the mouthpiece of AKEL, the Communist Party. Periodicals include the widely read *To Periodico* (*The Periodical*), established in 1986, which covers current events, lifestyle, politics, and fashion. *Xpress Economiki* is one of Cyprus's more popular electronic newspaper.

Popular English language papers include the daily *Cyprus Mail* and the popular weekly paper *Cyprus Weekly*. Although the latter has become increasingly anti-Turkish, both are renowned for their news coverage. *The Blue Beret*, published once every two months, is an English-language publication for the UN forces posted in Cyprus. There are newspapers that cater to specific interests. For example, sports enthusiasts read *Athlitiko Vimo* (*Sports Tribune*) and those interested in business can read the *Financial Mirror*. There are also local publications such as the *Famagusta Gazette* and *Phonitis Pafou* (*Voice of Paphos*).

There are eight daily newspapers and three weeklies published in North Cyprus. The Largest daily circulation newspapers are *Kibris*, and *Halkin Sesi*. These publications are of a general interest and include current news on local and international political events, crime, business, sports, opinions, as well as weather forecasts, and some entertainment columns. *Cyprus Today*, founded in 1991, is the major English-language weekly newspaper in North Cyprus. Another weekly title in North Cyprus is *Cyprus Observer*, which is also distributed in Great Britain and has a more political standpoint. Other English-language publications include the monthly magazine *Pan*, the *North Cyprus Monthly*, and the quarterly magazine *Turquoise*.

RADIO AND TELEVISION

The Cyprus Broadcasting Corporation (CyBC) began operations in 1957 and is Cyprus's public broadcasting service. Its four radio channels broadcast programs in Greek, English, Turkish, and Armenian. An international service also broadcasts in Greek, English, and Arabic, directed at the many overseas Cypriot communities who live all around the world.

More than 20 smaller radio stations operate across the island and many can be listened to live online via the Internet.

The CyBC runs three television stations—CyBC 1, CyBC 2, and RIK Sat, broadcasting in both Greek and Turkish. It also imports many English programs. Greek programs from the mainland can be received via satellite, as can international satellite channels such as CNN and Star TV. The British Forces Broadcasting Service from the British military base at Akrotiri can be received throughout the island.

In North Cyprus Bayrak Radio and Television Corporation or, in Turkish, *Bayrak Radyo Televizyon Kurumu* (BRTK), is the state-run broadcaster. From its station in Nicosia, BRTK broadcasts news, sports, arts, women's hour, talks, educational, cultural, entertainment, and other social events programs on both television and radio. The radio transmits on three channels—Channel I for broadcasts in Turkish, Channel II for foreign language programs (mainly English and Greek), and Channel III for music. Users can also access BRTK programs online.

A Turkish Cypriot shopkeeper watching television.

ARTS

Priest and religious icon painter
Kallinikos Stavrovouny with one
of his paintings.

CHAPTER 10

N ITS LONG AND TURBULENT HISTORY, Cyprus has played host to many different visitors. The impact of the Greek, Roman, Persian, Byzantine, and Ottoman civilizations, and the Crusaders is evident in the architecture and artistic remains on the island.

Traditional music and dance are the most important and most popular arts in Cyprus. They have changed little over the centuries because of the isolation of a predominantly rural population. On both sides of the border, the governments have made considerable efforts to protect the medieval and ancient heritage of the island. In the north, the Department of Antiquities has carried out restoration work. In the south, archaeological digs and restoration projects have been able to attract international aid, especially when linked to the development of tourism. For this reason, Paphos, Curium, and Amathus are well-excavated sites, while sites such as Soli in the north still require extensive work.

ANCIENT HERITAGE

Many of the best finds are in the island's various museums, including district museums in Larnaca, Limassol, and Paphos; the Pieredes Foundation Museum in Larnaca; and the Cyprus Museum in southern Nicosia. Unfortunately only a small portion of Cyprus's ancient heritage has remained on the island. Many art objects were removed by European archaeologists in the 19th and early 20th centuries, and are now found in museums all over the world.

Cyprus celebrates many different art forms, including traditional music, song, dance, handicrafts, painting, literature, and architecture. Cyprus is home to a vast ancient heritage that has been unearthed in archaeological digs over the years.

The ancient amphitheater at Curium.

Many figurines, some of very high quality, have survived from the Chalcolithic or Copper Stone period (3800—2800 B.C.). The figures, usually made from picrolite, a soft, blue-green stone, include outstanding anthropomorphic figures shaped like a cross or cruciforms, idols, and female fertility symbols. Copper items from the Bronze Age (2300—1050 B.C.) confirm the island's reputation for metal work. Many bronze items, especially jewelry and vessels, were discovered in the royal tombs at Salamis. Many beautiful handmade vases survive from this time. Terracotta figures, including toys and female fertility figures, date from the Archaic period (750—475 B.C.). This period was also remarkable for its beautiful, embossed gold plaques, and jewelry.

The Classical period between 510 and 323 B.C. produced some large sculpture. The figurines wore Greek dress and had beards, reflecting the influence of Persia, as Persians at that time were known to have a love of long beards. The figures include an impressive representation of Aphrodite of Soli, which has become a popular symbol of Cyprus. Hellenistic art shows Athenian and Alexandrian influences, especially in the statues of local rulers and officials. The gold and jewelry of this period are magnificent. The Roman period between 27 B.C. and A.D. 476 is most famous for mosaics. Excellent examples at Soli depict a waterfowl flanked by dolphins, and a swan enclosed by floral patterns. At Salamis there are mosaics of the river god Evrotas and partial remnants of a battle scene. At Curium fifth-century mosaics depict scenes from the Trojan War and Greek mythology, while others have animals and geometric shapes indicating growing Christian influences.

Ancient architecture includes the impressive sites of Curium, with its Roman-built temple of Apollo Hylates, and the temple of Aphrodite at

Amathus. The most impressive ancient remains are at Salamis, north of Famagusta. Most of the ruins at Salamis date from the Hellenistic, Roman, and Byzantine periods. They include a gymnasium, baths, amphitheater, and 150 royal tombs from the seventh and eighth centuries B.C.

MEDIEVAL ARCHITECTURE

Lusignan rule left a considerable architectural legacy in Cyprus. The Lusignans were a noble French family

Roman ruins at the ancient site of Salamis in northern Cyprus.

that was powerful around the 13th and 14th centuries. In 1192 Guy of Lusignan received the island of Cyprus from King Richard I of England. In 1194 Guy's brother, Amalric II, succeeded him as king of Cyprus. Cyprus flourished under Lusignan rule, and Nicosia was a center of French medieval culture. In 1375 the last Lusignan king of Armenia was overthrown by the Mamluks, and in 1489, the Lusignan dynasty finally ended with Venice taking complete control of Cyprus. The Lusignans introduced fine Gothic architecture at a time when Western Europe was achieving its architectural zenith. One of these buildings is the Selimiye Mosque, a former cathedral, in the heart of old Nicosia. Originally built as Saint Sophia Cathedral by French architects in 1209, its broad outline resembles some of the magnificent medieval cathedrals of France. Following the Ottoman occupation the cathedral was converted to a mosque in 1571 and all Christian decorations were removed.

Famagusta is home to some of the most impressive medieval architecture in the Middle East. The famous painter Leonardo da Vinci is said to have been involved in the construction of its Venetian-style fortifications. The walls of Famagusta have a squat appearance—in some places they are 49 feet (15 m) tall and 26 feet (8 m) thick.

A medieval structure in bright stone, the Kolossi Castle is surrounded by orchards.

Cyprus has numerous examples of Renaissance military architecture. Some of the most elaborate include the castles at Kyrenia, Saint Hilarion, Buffavento, and Kantara. These are all situated in the Kyrenia Mountains. Saint Hilarion castle, for example, was originally built by the Byzantines, mainly as a defense against Arab raiders and pirates. Nicosia's city walls contain a fascinating mixture of architecture that reflects the city's turbulent history. The walls were originally built by the Venetians in the 16th century. Although not high, they are extremely thick and were designed to allow cannons to be rolled along the ramparts.

Cyprus has many magnificent, isolated monasteries in the mountains. The ruins of Sourp Magar monastery are nestled amid the Kyrenia Mountains. Like many of the island's monasteries, it is a vestige of the Cypriot church's powerful and wealthy past. Antiphonitis monastery, which contains many exquisite frescoes, is one of the most architecturally impressive religious buildings in Cyprus. Other well-known monasteries include the Stavrovouni monastery, perched on a rocky crag to the west of Larnaca. The monastery has a long and illustrious history. Founded by Saint Helena in A.D. 327, the monastery is thought to have contained a fragment of the biblical True Cross. The monastery was burned in both Lusignan times and by the Ottomans. The present building dates from the 19th century.

The Kykko monastery in the Troodos Mountains and the monastery of Ayios Chrysostomos on the southern slopes of the Kyrenia range were built in the 11th century. They are classic examples of late Byzantine monastic architecture. The 13th-century abbey at Bellapais near Kyrenia boasts an impressive cloister, church, and magnificent refectory.

ICON PAINTING

A long-standing bastion of the Orthodox Christian religion, beautiful icons, and frescoes have been painted in the churches and monasteries of Cyprus since Byzantine times. Icons are the principal religious art form of the Orthodox faith, transmitting to the faithful the glory of God. Depictions of biblical scenes and scenes from liturgical history, and images of the Virgin Mary, Jesus, and the Apostles offer physical representations to inspire and direct the faith of worshipers.

An icon painter in Stavrovouni monastery at work.

Icons are not merely works of art, but are imbued with religious significance and venerated by the faithful. Literally hundreds of churches all over the island are intricately decorated with religious reliefs and icons.

Icon painting began in the early Byzantine period, in the sixth century. Cyprus became a refuge for icon painters during the eighth and ninth centuries, when there were doctrinal disputes over whether it was appropriate to worship images. Because of this theological controversy, icons were destroyed in great numbers. Many of the more impressive church paintings found today are derived from the later Byzantine period, in the 10th and 12th centuries. Many have faded beyond recognition, but some remarkable ones can still be found at Ayios Trypiotis in Nicosia, Ayios Lazaros in Larnaca, and the Apostolos Andreas monastery on the Karpas Peninsula. Some of the best icon painters in Europe practiced their art on the island, including the 14th-century master Philip Goul, who decorated the churches of Stavros tou Ayiasmati and Ayios Mamas at Louvaras, located high in the Troodos Mountains. Typical paintings depict scenes from the Bible, illustrating the lives of Jesus and the Apostles. In the chapel of Ayios Mamas, impressive frescoes depict Jesus healing the sick and blind, the Last Supper, and John the Baptist. Recently icons were collected in the Byzantine Museum in Nicosia and the Icon Museum in Kyrenia.

Icon painting is highly stylized. The subject is captured with a perfect visage, frozen for eternity. Naturalistic representations are rare. Today icon-making continues in the monasteries, expressing religious fervor and devotion.

MODERN PAINTING AND SCULPTURE

Modern art did not develop in Cyprus until the beginning of the 20th century, following trends in Europe. Since then Cypriot artists have sought to capture the moods and nuances of the landscape. One of Cyprus's better-known painters and sculptors, Christoforos Savva (1924—68), painted in an innovative post-Cubist style using sharp, magnificent colors. His most famous works are *Nude* (1957), and the abstract *Composition with Two Circles* (1967). Other leading Cypriot artists include Stass Paraskos, born in 1933, who is influenced by the island's artistic and archaeological heritage; the Constructivist Stelios Votsis, who was born in 1929; and the Expressionist Vera Hadjida, born in 1936. Andreas Savvides, born in 1930, has produced work that includes monumental sculptures and abstract compositions combining different materials.

LITERATURE

Modern Cypriot literature is not well established or widely read outside the island. One reason for this is that the Greek Cypriot dialect is different from the mainland language, making widespread distribution of Greek Cypriot writing very difficult. Among writers on both sides of the divide, poetry is the most popular medium of expression. Political-literary magazines, such as the left-wing *Nea Epochi* (*New Epoch*) and the literary monthly *Pnevmatiki Kypros* (*Intellectual Cyprus*), indicate the vibrancy of Greek Cypriots' interest in modern literature.

The Turkish victory monument in Famagusta is one of many sculptures in Cyprus commemorating the people who have perished in the clashes between Greeks and Turks over the years.

HANDICRAFTS

Folk art is still alive and well in Cyprus, and weaving and lacework are still a part of the lives of many Cypriot women, especially in the villages. It has been argued that Cypriot arts and crafts have their origin in the need of young women to be provided with a dowry. Men would craft objects from copper, gourds, and wood. Mothers and daughters would also produce great quantities of embroidered linen for the bride's dowry, to provide bed sheets, pillowcases, furniture coverings, towels, and floor covers. Today the picturesque village of Lefkara, in the foothills of the Troodos Mountains west of Larnaca, is the center of this craft tradition, famous for its lace embroidery and silver creations.

Although Lefkara's lace industry prospers, the same cannot be said for other cottage industries in Cyprus. High-quality pottery and ceramics, for example, have been produced in Cyprus for many centuries, but producers have found themselves unable to compete internationally. In the past *pitharia* (PIH-thah-ree-ah), containers three feet (about one meter) in diameter and made by highly regarded craftsmen, were produced for storing olive oil, olives, and wine. Today they are often used to hold flowers in gardens. Small pottery, including glazed vases, figurines, bowls, and pitchers, is the specialty of the Paphos district. These are often decorated with floral patterns or geometric designs reminiscent of their ancient counterparts. Gourd flasks have also been made for centuries, although they are not often used today. Wickerwork and basketry are also common.

DANCE AND SONG

In Cyprus music and dance are traditionally the most popular art forms. Today traditional forms are threatened by disco and pop music, especially Greek pop music, which is increasingly played on many festive occasions. Most Cypriot boys and girls learn to dance both traditional and modern variations of dances at school. Some purists believe that although dance classes in school are useful to ensure a wide knowledge of Cypriot dance, the classes also limit the spontaneity of the performers by encouraging uniformity of movement.

Dances are usually performed on special occasions, such as at weddings, or on festival days. In the past men would dance not only on festive occasions, but also in coffeehouses in the evening, or even on the threshing floor. Today the occasions for dancing are more restricted. There are many kinds of Cypriot dances, most of which can be performed by both men and women. Traditionally men danced with men, and women with women. The only exception was when the bride danced with the groom at a wedding party. More recently mixed dancing has been introduced, although traditionalists frown on such developments.

Stylistically men's dances are usually more lively, while women's dances are more delicate and restrained. The best-known dance is the *kartchilamas* (gar-chee-LAH-mahs), performed by pairs of male and female dancers. Often this will form the foundation for a much broader suite, rounded off with more complicated dances such as the *syrtos* (SEE-tohs) and *mandra* (MAHN-drah). The *syrtos* is a particularly popular dance at social gatherings, such as weddings. The *kartchilamas*, a very lively dance, offers the men the opportunity to compete with each other and demonstrate their strength, while the women's dances tend to stress restraint and grace. Stamping feet on one spot is a typical feature of the *kartchilamas* and the *syrtos*. The *dhrepanin* (threh-PAH-neen), or "sickle dance," has an agricultural theme, where the male dancers cut imaginary swathes in the air and around their bodies as they mow the harvest. This dance is particularly popular at the festival Kataklismós, and allows male dancers to express themselves energetically. In the women's dances, the woman stays in one spot, and much of the movement is in the positioning of the arms and the turning of the body.

Cypriots take great pride in their traditional folk songs. Love songs, working songs, children's rhymes, humorous songs, wedding songs, laments, and political rhymes are all part of the Cypriot canon. The most popular rhythm is the *kalamatianos* (gar-LAH-mah-tee-ah-nohs), a tempo with ancient origins.

In its purest and most traditional form, music is played on a shepherd's flute, or *auloi* (ow-LOH-ee). The violin and flute are used to accompany dance performances. Another traditional instrument is the *laoudo* (LAH-oo-doh), or long-necked flute. Turkish traditional instruments include the *zorna* (zoh-NAH), a kind of oboe; the *davul* (dah-VUHL), a two-headed drum; and the *kasat* (kah-SAHT), or small finger cymbals. But with a rising appetite for modern pop music, traditional music and instruments are in decline.

A medieval-style musician playing outside a castle wall.

LEISURE

A man cliff jumping on Nissi Island, in Agia Napa in southern Cyprus.

A S A POPULAR HOLIDAY DESTINATION, modern Cyprus is, in the minds of many people, associated with leisure.

This is an image that the casual Cypriots are happy to cultivate. Sitting, drinking, and eating with friends, whether in a restaurant, or coffee shop, remain the most popular and traditional ways to relax for most Cypriots. Backgammon, an ancient game played in this part of the world, is the most common indoor game. It is played by men almost everywhere on the island.

The island's warm and dry climate, rugged landscape, and varied coastline have resulted in Cyprus gaining a reputation as an outdoor sports paradise. It is also an excellent place to engage in water sports.

Elderly men play backgammon, one of the most popular games in Cyprus.

Cypriots value and enjoy their leisure time. They take great pleasure in socializing with friends and family at home or in the local tavern. Visitors come to Cyprus to enjoy the many leisure and sporting activities that are available.

Other activities, such as mountain biking, cycling, and hiking, have become extremely popular with visitors to Cyprus. Golf is also heavily promoted. Traditional sports, such as soccer and hunting, remain predominant among the local people.

RURAL PURSUITS

Cyprus's warm climate makes it an ideal location for outdoor activities. Family picnics on Sundays or festival days are popular. The whole family will travel to the coast or the countryside and eat kebabs in the shade of an olive tree. The low temperatures in the Troodos Mountains make the area an ideal place to relax.

Nature trails have been marked recently along the coast and in the mountains. Hikers, often tourists, can easily follow signs that give details about the local flora and fauna in Greek and English.

Cyprus's climate makes engaging in outdoor activities, like cycling, very enjoyable.

Cyprus boasts of one leisure activity that is considered exotic in the Middle East—skiing. There is a ski resort on the northeastern face of Mount Olympus in the Troodos Mountains. It is open from January to early April. An international ski event—the Troodos International FIS Ski Race—which attracts top skiers from around the world, is held in February or March.

HUNTING

The hunting of small game and birds has traditionally been popular in Cyprus. In the 1970s it was estimated that as many as 10 million birds were killed each year in Cyprus—more than 15 birds for every man, woman, and child on the island! Although this number has since decreased, and some species have become protected in nature reserves, hunting remains popular. The hills around the village of Dipkarpas on the Karpas Peninsula are considered the best spot on the island for hunting of birds. In the hunting season, which lasts from November to January, the sport is so popular that men travel from Morphou, which is at the other end of the island, to participate. The catch is normally taken home and cooked. Hares and rabbits are also hunted. Since joining the EU in 2004, Cyprus has come under pressure to reinforce its bird protection laws. Although these bird protection laws are in place, illegal bird hunting continues to take place, with an estimated 3.2 million birds killed illegally every year.

BEACH LIFE

Cyprus adheres to the "Blue Flag Program," which promotes clean and environmentally friendly beaches. There are several Blue Flag beaches located around the southern coastline. In the north, there are some outstanding, secluded coves and bays for swimming. The stretch of Famagusta Bay, for example, is considered one of the finest beaches in the Mediterranean. There are also many small beaches along the northern coast to the west and east of Kyrenia. Popular beaches include those at Lara Bay and Alakati. The former is famous as a breeding ground for loggerhead turtles and a vital environmental resource—during the breeding season, the beach is reserved for turtles. Other beaches along the northern coast are used by the North Cypriots, and on the weekends they become crowded with families having barbecues and enjoying the sea air. The southern coastline of the Karpas Peninsula has some of the island's most beautiful, inaccessible, and unspoiled beaches. Here the Nangomí beach, which runs for three miles (4.8 km), is probably the best—and cleanest—beach on the entire island, with not a soft drink bottle or *taverna*—a café or small restaurant—in sight.

Many of the tourist beaches in the south have been artificially created, especially around Limassol and Paphos, where the shore has been improved with sand brought from elsewhere. Other good beaches include Governor's Beach, 20 miles (32 km) east of Limassol; and Pissouri Beach, west of the British base at Episkopi. While the beaches around Ayia Napa provide some good stretches of sand, every inch is filled by the many thousands of tourists who visit this area. Although the beaches in the south are of a poorer quality, they tend to have more facilities, with water sports, beach-side tavernas, drink vendors, beach furniture, and children's playgrounds all provided.

The best beach used to be at Glossa, to the south of Varosha. Now it is deserted, a result of the evacuation of Varosha in 1974.

Fig Tree Bay in Protatas. Beaches in Cyprus are hives of activity.

Cypriots enjoy spending time chatting over food at taverns or restaurants.

Throughout the south, it is difficult to find the seclusion that defines the north. The exception is the isolated and often off-limits Akamas peninsula, where a number of excellent unspoiled beaches remain, protected by British military rights to practice bombing and firing.

The island's huge tourist industry has led to an explosion of water and beach sports, including windsurfing, waterskiing, speed boating, dinghy sailing, jetskiing, scuba diving, and parasailing. Some beaches even have bungee-jumping facilities. These activities are based around the hotels and are most popular with tourists and expatriates. The capes near Paphos, Ayia Napa, and Protaras are the most popular spots for windsurfing, while sailing is popular in the bays off Larnaca and Limassol. Diving is popular in waters all around the island, thanks to the crystal-clear water and rocky coastline. Submarine cliffs and valleys, coral, and exotic sea life provide plenty of underwater attractions for divers.

CITY FUN

Traditionally Cypriots of all ages spend their time chatting over food and drinks for the whole evening in their favorite taverna or restaurant.

Turkish baths can be found in many parts of the Middle East and eastern Mediterranean, and in many of the cities of Cyprus. One of the largest and best-known, the Büyük Hammam, which means "the Grand Baths," lies in northern Nicosia. It provides traditional Turkish baths. Fridays are reserved for women, but all other days are for men only. The treatment includes an exposure to warm air, then steam, followed by a massage, and finally a cold shower. Most baths have separate washrooms and soaking pools.

Bathers spend many happy hours sweating in the hot rooms, followed by washing with a camel hair glove, or perhaps a vigorous massage by a masseur. The bath is considered an excellent way to lose weight, cleanse the skin, and generally relax the mind and body. Those who believe in the medicinal qualities of the Turkish bath try to visit as often as possible—at least once a month, or even once a week.

Like many aspects of island life, soccer has become a symbol of the divisions and differences. Cyprus has had two separate soccer federations since 1955. The Republic of Cyprus refuses to recognize any teams from the north, and vice versa.

Although Cypriots tend to avoid the resort areas such as Ayia Napa, many young Cypriots enjoy the night life of Nicosia, Limassol, and Paphos. The rapid expansion of the island's tourist scene has led to an explosion of clubs, bars, and restaurants in the main tourist areas. Nightclubs, bars, and pubs have only been recently introduced to Cyprus. They tend to be patronized by the young and more liberal-minded Cypriots.

Movies are also popular in Cyprus, especially international and American ones. These films usually have Greek or Turkish subtitles, depending on which side of the border they are shown. Big movie-houses pack in moviegoers in Nicosia, Larnaca, and Limassol.

SPORTS

Soccer remains the most popular sport on the island, both north and south of the divide, and attracts more spectators than any other sport. Recently teams such as Anorthosis Famagusta and Apoel Nicosia have advanced to the group stage of the UEFA Champions League, the highest club-level competition in Europe. Cypriots also like tennis, both as players and spectators, and courts in the hotels and public areas of the towns in the south are always booked. A well-known Greek Cypriot tennis player is Markos Baghdatis, who advanced to the Australian Open final and the Wimbledon semifinals in 2006. In that same year, he was ranked number eight in the world.

Although Cyprus is not at the forefront of world athletics, the island has strong athletic traditions, stretching back to the time of the ancient Greeks. Cypriots are also thought to have participated in the earliest Olympic games. With the Ottoman occupation and arrival of the Turks, weightlifting was encouraged as the national sport.

Every September the Cyprus Car Rally attracts entries from many world-class championship drivers. The winding tracks and rugged landscape offer competitors a tough test of their driving abilities.

The love for soccer has been passed from one generation to the next. From an early age, Cypriot boys learn how to play soccer.

FESTIVALS

A girl at the Anthesteria Flower Festival held in Limassol.

I N THE GREEK SOUTH, PUBLIC HOLIDAYS and festivals tend to have a religious focus, reflecting the dominant position of the Orthodox Church in Greek Cypriot culture.

Recently tourist authorities have organized many special events to attract foreigners. In the north, which is a secular society, people celebrate significant events in Turkish Cypriot communal history and a few imported festivals from the mainland.

Although there are many major islandwide festivals, celebrating local village festivals remains a strong tradition. Feast days of the local

A young girl receives blessings from a priest.

saints provide Cypriots with a good excuse for a party. Traditionally this would always have occurred in the village, and many town dwellers would return to their ancestral village to participate in local festivals. However, with increased urbanization, city festivals have become more important.

GREEK ORTHODOX FESTIVALS

Among Greek Cypriots the Orthodox religion plays a central role in the history, identity, and life of the community. Many age-old pagan festivals have over the centuries been given an Orthodox interpretation, while maintaining notable pagan elements. New Year's Day, for example, is celebrated with the Feast of Ayios Vasílios, or Saint Basil (A.D. 329—79), one of the spiritual fathers of the Orthodox church who is respected throughout the Orthodox world. Saint Basil is the Cypriot equivalent of Santa Claus. Gifts are exchanged on this day rather than Christmas.

Epiphany on January 6 marks the baptism of Christ in the River Jordan. It is called *Fóta* (FOH-tah) by Cypriots, meaning "illumination." On this day

A priest passes around the flame. It is considered good luck to arrive home with the candle still alight, and to trace a sooty sign of the cross over the threshold of the home.

holy water fonts in churches are blessed to banish the evil spirits that are said to have lurked on Earth since Christmas. The festival is also marked by the baking of doughnuts. It is customary to throw the first doughnut on the roof of the house to scare away any lingering evil spirits. In seaside towns, the celebration reaches a finale when the local bishop throws a crucifix far out into the water and young men swim for the honor of recovering it. March 25 fulfills the dual function of celebrating Greek Independence Day and the feast of the Annunciation.

Easter is the most important celebration in the Greek Orthodox calendar. Many festivals are linked to the Easter festivities. Green Monday, a pre-Lenten carnival, lasts for 10 days in early March. The celebration is held in Limassol and kicks off with the carnival king's entrance to the town on a float, followed by fancy-dress parades, games, and much feasting. After Green Monday, Easter observances begin with Lenten fasting for a full 50 days.

Orthodox Good Friday is marked by processions through the villages led by a coffin containing a figure of Christ. The difference in timing between Western

A family celebrates Orthodox Easter Sunday with a barbecue.

and Eastern churches in celebrating Easter can range from the same day to up to four weeks. Village women prepare elaborate floral decorations for the funeral bier. Every icon is draped in black cloth to mark the crucifixion. On Saturday night huge bonfires are lit, and villagers gather in the local church to celebrate the Jesus Christ's resurrection. Everyone holds a candle, while children hold sparklers. At midnight the priest announces Christ's resurrection and eternal life for all believers. The priest passes around a lighted flame, which is handed from worshiper to worshiper. The Lenten fast is broken immediately after the service, with the eating of egg and lemon soup and the cracking of dyed eggs. On Easter Sunday preparations

On Assumption Day (August 15) and Saint Andrew's Day (November 30) many pilgrims—both Christians and Muslims—pay a visit to the Apostolos Andreas monastery (monastery of Saint Andrew), near the tip of the Karpas peninsula. The monastery has a reputation as the "Lourdes" of Cyprus, where pilgrims seek cures for their afflictions. This reputation stems from a visit to the spot made by the apostle Saint Andrew, the great miracle worker and protector of travelers. He is thought to have stopped here to fetch water while on a trip to preach Christianity in Greece. After restoring the sight of the one-eyed captain of his ship with the local water, Saint Andrew is said to have converted and baptized the crew. As a result a chapel was built in the 15th century at the tiny spring in a nearby rock grotto thought to have healing powers. For many years, it was rumored that the site could heal blindness, deafness, and illnesses of all kinds.

get under way for the baking of special holiday cakes, called *flaoúnes* (flah-OON-ehs), a pastry filled with egg, cheese, and raisins.

The Festival of the Flood, or *Kataklismós* (kaht-ah-klees-MOHS), is unique to Cyprus and is celebrated seven weeks after Easter. Elsewhere in the Orthodox world it is merely Pentecost, but in Cyprus it becomes a week-long celebration, especially in coastal towns.

The Assumption of the Virgin, on August 15, marks the rise to heaven of the Virgin Mary and is an important Orthodox festival. The day is celebrated with fairs in many villages and monasteries. Christmas is a far less important holiday in the Orthodox Church, and is relatively subdued in Cyprus. Western-style commercialization has changed Christmas celebrations in recent years, and it is now more common to give and receive presents. The most durable traditional custom is the singing of carols—children go door-to-door, singing, accompanied by a triangle.

Other Orthodox festivals are also celebrated—Saint Anthony's Day, which honors the Egyptian father of the monastic life, is marked in Nicosia and Limassol on January 17, while Saint George's Day on April 23 is celebrated almost everywhere on the island. Apart from islandwide Orthodox festivals, many other celebrations are held locally throughout Cyprus, to honor the local

During the Festival of the Flood, people crowd into the sea and sprinkle one another with water, to commemorate the salvation of Noah and the ark from the biblical floods.

patron saint or holy figure of a monastery. These include the Erection of the Holy Cross at the Stavrovouni monastery in Larnaca on September 14, and the celebration of Saints Peter and Paul in Paphos on June 29, which is attended by the archbishop and other bishops of the island. Saint Neophytos's Day (January 24), which honors the Cypriot religious figure, is celebrated with a massive procession that ends at the famous hermit's cave north of Paphos.

MUSLIM FESTIVALS

In North Cyprus all major Islamic festivals are celebrated according to the lunar calendar, meaning that the festival recedes by 11 days each year. *Seker Bayrami* (sheh-kehr bay-rah-MIH), meaning "the sugar festival," because of the great amount of sweets eaten at this time, is celebrated at the end of the fasting month, Ramadan. This three-day holiday is commonly celebrated with a family get-together and the distribution of sweets and presents to the children. *Kurban Bayrami* (kehr-bahn bay-rah-MIH), the Feast of the Sacrifice,

Shopping for sweets before the sugar festival.

Although Turkish Cypriots celebrate major Muslim festivals, they are not as strict in their observances as some of their neighbors in the Middle East.

commemorates Abraham's willingness to sacrifice his son, and usually occurs two months after Seker Bayrami. Traditionally families sacrifice a sheep or chicken, which is then eaten at a large family gathering. Kurban Bayrami is usually a four-day national holiday, the longest of the year. The Muslim new year and *Mevlúd* (mehv-LUHD), or the birth of the Prophet Muhammad, are also celebrated.

NONRELIGIOUS FESTIVALS

THE REPUBLIC OF CYPRUS hosts many nonreligious festivals, especially in the summer. Although some of these celebrations have a traditional or pagan origin, many of them have been revamped and promoted by the tourist authorities to attract ever-increasing numbers of visitors. The most important city festival in Cyprus is the Limassol Wine Festival, held for around 10 days every September. The city's municipal gardens become the site for contemporary merrymaking, where visitors pay an entrance fee that

Girls participating at the Anthesteria Flower Festival in Germansogeia in Limassol.

entitles them to sample any of the wines available and attend all the musical and theatrical activities. All the island's wineries take part, offering wine to all who want it. Beer festivals are also organized. During these festivals beer is sold at a reduced price and is consumed along with Cypriot snacks, accompanied by traditional dancing and music.

In May virtually every town holds a flower festival. The festivities include colorful processions though the streets and competitions for the best flower arrangements. Harvest festivals are also a common feature in some of the larger villages on the island. The whole district will celebrate with singing, feasting, and dancing in the village square. The more tourist-oriented Paphos Festival of Ancient Greek Drama is staged in the medieval castle and ancient odeon theater of the town in the summer months. Paphos also organizes the popular Paphos Carnival and Akamas Festival of classical music. Limassol hosts an International Arts Festival in June and July. The Curium Drama Festival takes place in July and August. Overlooking the sea, the 2,000-year-old theater at Curium provides a spectacular setting for the staging of ancient Greek dramas and works by Shakespeare and modern dramatists.

On October 1 Cyprus's Independence Day is celebrated to mark the island's independence, while Greek Independence Day is celebrated on March 25, in solidarity with their brethren on the mainland.

THE TURKISH NORTH In the north many official holidays have been imported from the Turkish mainland. However, unlike in the south, there simply is no budget to hold large and lavish celebrations. Thus most festivals are low-key affairs. Many Turkish Cypriot holidays mark significant events in the Turkish struggle against the Greek desire for enosis, such as TMT Day, or the birth of Turkish Cypriot resistance, on August 1, as well as political events such as the 1974 invasion. The festival commemorating the invasion is called Peace and Freedom Day, and falls on July 20. Harvest festivals in the villages on the Mesaoria Plain are probably the liveliest events, celebrated to mark the harvesting of the orange, strawberry, and watermelon crops.

FOOD

A man grills quail at a taverna in southern Cyprus.

C YPRIOT FOOD IS GENERALLY considered hearty rather than refined, with an emphasis on a wide variety of simple and tasty, home-cooked fare. It reflects a broad range of influences that are the product of Cyprus's history and geographic location. Middle Eastern, southern European, and British influences can all be detected.

Cypriot food draws most strongly on the culinary traditions of Greece and Turkey, from which most of the dishes derive. Lamb and chicken

A group of men sits outside a café, having some drinks.

For Cypriots food and drink are an essential part of every social occasion, whether it is a wedding, festival, family gathering, or meeting between friends. Virtually every conversation and meeting is accompanied by coffee, beer or brandy, and snacks.

are the most popular meats, and seafood is also widely eaten. Grilling and frying are the usual methods of cooking. Olive oil is used generously in Cypriot cuisine, for both cooking and garnishing. Almost all meals are eaten with bread, fried or grilled vegetables, and salad.

THE GREEK CYPRIOT TABLE

Traditionally Cypriots ate a simple rural diet of bread, olives, and yogurt, accompanied by cheese, tomatoes, and cucumbers. The dish was drizzled with salt, olive oil, and lemon. Today Cyprus's new found wealth has resulted in a richer, more varied diet for most Cypriots.

Meat is usually the highlight of any Greek Cypriot meal. Game, including duck, pigeon, quail, and rabbit, is the favorite, but it is only eaten on special occasions. *Souvlakia* (soov-LAH-kee-yah), or lamb roasted on a spit, often forms the culinary focus of any big gathering. *Kleftikó* (glehf-tee-KOH), which is lamb or goat roasted with an assortment of vegetables in an outdoor oven, is probably the closest thing to a national dish on the island.

Greek salad accompanies most meals and consists of cabbage, lettuce, celery, cucumbers, tomatoes, peppers, olives, feta cheese, and herbs, roughly chopped and mixed together.

There is no particular order to eating Greek Cypriot cuisine, although sweets are usually eaten last.

Every farmhouse and many other houses will have an outdoor oven for the preparation of this dish. Sausages, another popular choice, come in various forms—*sheftalia* (shehf-TAHL-yah) is grilled sausage made from ground meat, while *pastourmas* (past-oor-MAHS) is a garlic sausage made from pork. The classic Greek Cypriot meat dish is *souvlaki* (soov-LAHK-ee), a kebab made of small cubes of grilled lamb on skewers, often garnished with lemon and salt. Fried meatballs, or *keftedes* (kehf-TEH-dehs), complete the typical Cypriot meat selection.

Bread is an essential part of the Cypriot meal and is always first served as a complement to the expected courses. The *pitta* (PEE-tah)—a flat, crescent-shaped, hollow bread—is most often eaten filled with salad or vegetables and *souvlakia*. Vegetable dishes are usually either grilled or fried in oil, garnished with herbs, and mixed with a little tomato and olive oil. Favorites include stuffed or plain *kolokithakia* (koh-loh-kee-THA-kyah) or squash, *koukia* (koo-KYAH) or broad beans, and *koupepia* (koo-PEH-pyah) or vine leaves

MEZE

Cypriots love to share a mixture of as many assorted dishes as possible. This style of dining is known as meze (meh-ZEE), meaning "mixture." Meze is the most popular way of entertaining in the home, and is a feature of every restaurant and tavern menu. Meze usually includes a little of everything that is in the kitchen that day. In this way, it provides an excellent introduction to Cypriot cooking. A typical meze will usually include fried or grilled fish, keftedes and other kinds of kebabs, sheftalia, pastourmas, hirómeri (hee-ROH-meh-ree) or cured local ham, calamari (fried squid rings), hummos, taramas, tahini, Greek salad, beans, pickled cauliflower, olives, any number of vegetable dishes, and great quantities of bread. Often, a few Cypriot specialties will be included, in particular halumi (hah-LOO-mih), a rubbery goat cheese that is often served grilled or just eaten simply with bread and salad. It tastes especially good when fried. The great quantity of food and the vast array of tastes represent a test of appetite and endurance for even the most enthusiastic diner. This, more than any reason, is why Cypriots linger so long over their meals. The whole meal will be washed down with plenty of wine or beer.

filled with rice and formed into rolls. *Moussakas* (moo-sah-KAHS)—layered ground beef, potatoes, and slices of eggplant, baked in a white sauce with a cheese topping—is popular.

Cyprus has a number of puréed dips that can be eaten either with a full meal or as a snack, usually with pitta bread. These include *hummos* (HOO-mohs), or chickpeas puréed and mixed with garlic and lemon; *taramas* (tah-rah-MAHS), a pink, fish roe pâté made with potato purée, lemon, and onions; *talatoúra* (tah-lah-TOO-rah), a yogurt, cucumber, and herb dip that is very cooling and especially good with spicy meat dishes; and *tahini* (tah-HEE-nee), or sesame seed paste.

Although Cypriots are less inclined to eat snacks compared to their mainland Greek and Turkish counterparts, baked tidbits are popular. In the south, these include *kolokótes* (koh-loh-KOH-tehs), a triangular pastry stuffed with pumpkin, cracked wheat, and raisins; *takhino pitta* (tah-chee-NOH-pee-tah), a pastry with sesame paste; and *eliópitta* (ehl-YOH-pee-tah), an olive turnover.

A man holds up loaves of freshly baked bread. Bread is an integral part of Cypriot cuisine.

So much time is given to the pleasures of eating, it is a wonder that Cypriots find time for any other business.

TURKISH CUISINE

Turkish Cypriot cuisine owes its heritage to a mixture of Middle Eastern and southern European influences. Although it has the same fundamental characteristics as Greek Cypriot food, since the partition, the food in the north has become increasingly influenced by mainland tastes. As in the republic, meze, including Turkish variations such as hummus, *tarama*, tahini, and *cacik* (jah-CHIK) or *talatoúra*, is extremely popular. Other more typical Turkish dishes include *yalanci dolma* (yah-lahn-CHI dohl-MAH), similar to *koupepia*, where vine leaves are stuffed with rice, onions, and tomatoes; *musakka* (moo-sah-KAH), similar to the Greek Cypriot dish; and *lazböregi* (lahz-behr-reh-YEH), or meat-filled crepes topped with yogurt. Turkish kebabs come in many varieties, including the ubiquitous shish kebab, or marinated lamb skewered and grilled over charcoal; and the *köfte* (kehrf-TEH), or spiced meatballs. Seafood is also popular. Fresh lobster, crab, mussels, squid, rock bream, and sea bass can be found in the north, although they are expensive.

Salads and vegetable dishes typically include tomatoes, eggplant, red onions, cucumbers, peppers, olives, and radishes. *Fasulye piyaz* (fahs-uhl-YEH pih-YAHZ), a green bean salad topped with olives and hard-boiled eggs, is a common accompaniment to meals or as part of a meze. The curiously named *imam bayaldi* (ih-MAHM bah-yahl-DIH), meaning "the imam fainted," is a traditional dish of baked eggplant cut in strips and stuffed with onions, garlic, and tomatoes. Street vendors sell *börek* (behr-EHK), a rich, flaky pastry containing bits of meat or cheese. Homemade and sold on the street, *börek* is the pride of Turkish Cypriot cuisine.

SWEETS

Cypriot desserts tend to be extremely sweet and are usually made with local fruit, honey, syrup, and pastry. *Soudzoúkou* (sood-ZOO-koo), a confection of almonds strung together and dipped in grape molasses and rosewater, are sold everywhere. *Baklavas* (pah-klah-VAHS) is the classic Cypriot sweet, made of filo pastry layers alternating with honey and nuts. *Daktila* (dahk-

Homemade almond sweets, *soudzoúkou*.

tee-LAH), a finger-shaped strudel pastry filled with cinnamon and dipped in syrup, is also common. *Halvas* (hahl-VAHS) is a sweet made from a grainy paste of semolina or tahini, while *loukoumades* (loo-koo-MAH-dehs) consists of deep-fried balls of choux pastry served in syrup. *Glyká* (glee-KAH) is a kind of preserved candied fruit, made with either cherries, oranges, or figs, usually only made at village festivals. The Paphos district is famous for *loukoumia* (loo-koo-MYAH), or cubes of gelatin served in rosewater and covered with powdered sugar.

FRUIT

Cypriot fruit has a well-deserved reputation for tastiness. Fruit is sold in roadside stalls and in all the town bazaars. The warm climate and long growing season means that Cypriot varieties tend to arrive at the market

A fruit and vegetable stall at the Wednesday market in Nicosia.

well before their counterparts in Europe, usually in April. In the south, strawberries are available all year-round. Peaches, apricots, watermelon, and desert melons are also grown, as are plums and cherries. The many varieties of cherries grown on the foothills of the Troodos Mountains are delicious. Grapes appear in the early autumn, a by-product of the republic's successful wine industry. Apples, pears, figs, almonds, cherries, lemons, and oranges are also used in Cypriot cooking. Exotic fruit not native to Cyprus, such as avocados, bananas, and kiwis, have been introduced to the warmer corners of the Paphos district. Despite the importance of agriculture to the northern economy, much of the fruit is imported from Turkey, partly because of the inefficiency and backwardness of local farming methods.

DRINKS

A feature of island life since the Ottoman invasion is Turkish coffee—*kafés* (kah-FEHS) in Greek, *kahve* (kah-VEH) in Turkish. It is widely drunk on both sides of the partition, though in the south it is generally referred to as Greek or Cypriot coffee, despite its Turkish origins. The fine ground coffee is boiled, then poured straight into a small cup without filtering and drunk either with sugar or straight, leaving a muddy residue at the bottom of the cup. Ideally, it is said that coffee should be drunk as sweet as sin, as hot as hell, and as dark as night. Since the arrival of settlers from Anatolia, the custom of brewing loose-leafed tea is becoming more popular in the villages of the north. Otherwise tea is not a popular drink. Cyprus also produces its own mineral water—the Troodos and Kyrenia mountains are both famous for their mountain springs, and some water is bottled and sold islandwide. Another popular drink sold by street vendors in Nicosia and Larnaca is *aïráni* (ah-ee-RAHN-ee), a refreshing concoction of diluted yogurt mixed with dried mint or oregano.

Traditionally Cypriots only drink alcohol to accompany a meal. Wine is normally drunk with meals in the day, even for breakfast, while on special occasions beer and brandy will be drunk. The wine of the south is of a very high standard, owing to the island's near-perfect climate and the long tradition of wine-making. Most of the vineyards are on the slopes of the Troodos Mountains, around Paphos and Limassol. Today Cyprus ranks 37th in the world in terms of total production of wine. The wine industry contributes significantly to Cyprus's economy. Many Cypriot families are employed in the wine industry, and Cyprus's many varieties of wine are exported all over the world. The best varieties of wine include the dry white varieties Arsinoë, Palomino, and White Lady, and the Bellapais medium sparkling wine. Among red wines, Othello and Rosella are common table wines. Commandaria is the most famous wine on the island. It is produced using the age-old method of fermentation in open jars. The same jars are repeatedly used, so that each new batch contains a trace of traditional quality.

It is said that in 1570 the Turkish sultan Selim was so intoxicated by his desire for the wine that he launched the Ottoman invasion on the island. Sherries are also produced, the most famous being the Emva brand. Local wine is also made in microwineries in the villages and monasteries of the Troodos, and drunk from the barrel.

Cyprus has a long tradition of wine-making and is known for its quality wine.

KEFTEDES (GREEK MEATBALLS)

2 pounds (1 kg) minced beef

2 onions, grated

2 eggs

1 teacup of olive oil

2—3 slices of bread

2 tablespoons (30 ml) chopped parsley

1 clove garlic

Salt and pepper

Oil for frying

Flour for coating

Place the minced beef in a bowl. Add the eggs, the parsley, the garlic, and the grated onion. Soak the bread and squeeze out excess moisture. Add the bread to the beef mixture along with salt and pepper. Mix all the ingredients well.

Make small round shapes and flatten them by hand until they are about ½ inch (1 cm) thick. Coat the meatballs lightly with flour. Heat a frying pan with olive oil and fry the meatballs until cooked.

Serve hot or cold.

YAYLA CORBASI (YOGURT SOUP)

6 cups (1.5 L) water

1 cube beef bouillon

½ cup (125 ml) rice, washed and drained

2 cups (500 ml) yogurt

½ cup (125 ml) milk

1 egg yolk

½ cup (125 ml) flour

2 tablespoons (30 ml) butter

1 tablespoon (15 ml) dry mint

Salt

In a large pot boil the water, rice, salt, and bouillon. Cook on medium high, until the rice is done.

Meanwhile, in a bowl, mix yogurt, milk, egg yolk, and flour. After the rice is cooked, take a few spoons of liquid from the pot and mix into the bowl. Then slowly pour the mixture into the pot while stirring very slowly. Cook for 10 more minutes.

Place the butter in a frying pan. When it begins spitting, stir in the mint, and pour it into the soup.

Serve immediately.

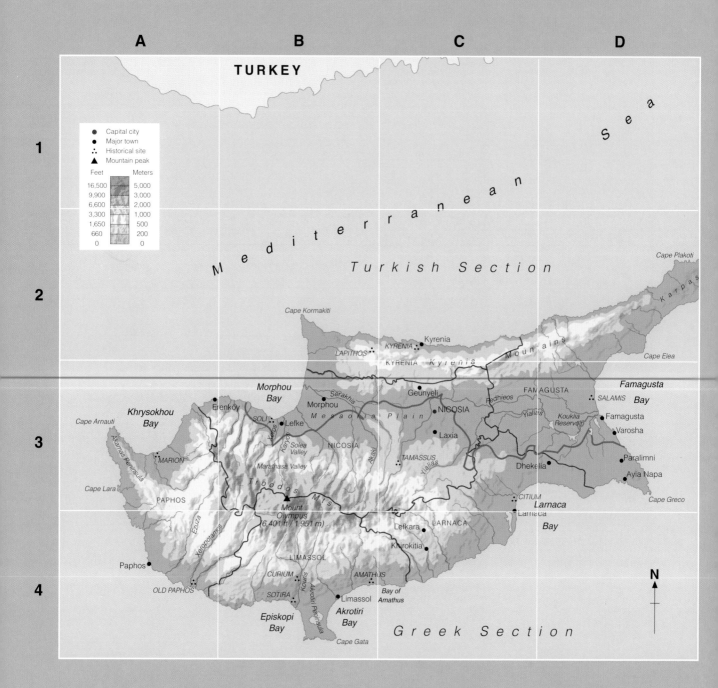

A **B** **C** **D**

TURKEY

1

Capital city
Major town
Historical site
Mountain peak

Feet	Meters
16,500	5,000
9,900	3,000
6,600	2,000
3,300	1,000
1,650	500
660	200
0	0

M e d i t e r r a n e a n   *S e a*

T u r k i s h   S e c t i o n

Cape Plakoti

2

Cape Kormakiti

Karpas

KYRENIA
LAPITHOS •Kyrenia
Kyrenia   *Mountains*

Cape Elea

KYRENIA

*Morphou
Bay*

*Famagusta
Bay*

*Khrysokhou
Bay*

Erenköy   Morphou   Serakhis
SOLI   •Lefke   *M e s a o r i a   P l a i n*   Geunyeli   FAMAGUSTA
Cape Arnauti   *Kargel*   Pedhieos   SALAMIS
•NICOSIA   Famagusta
3   *Akamas Peninsula*   *Solea
Valley*   NICOSIA   Laxia   Yialias   Kouklia   Varosha
•MARION   *Marathasa Valley*   *Akaki*   TAMASSUS   Paralimni
Cape Lara   *Yialias*   Dhekelia   Ayia Napa
PAPHOS   *Troodos   Mts.*   CITIUM   Cape Greco
Mount   *Ezusa*   Olympus   LARNACA   **Larnaca**
(6,401 ft / 1,951 m)   Lefkara   Larnaca
Paphos   *Xeropotamos*   *Bay*
OLD PAPHOS   LIMASSOL   Khirokitia
4   CURIUM   AMATHUS   Bay of
SOTIRA   *Kryos*   Amathus   **N**
*Episkopi
Bay*   *Akrotiri Peninsula*   *Akrotiri
Bay*   Limassol   *G r e e k   S e c t i o n*
Cape Gata

MAP OF CYPRUS

E

Cape Andreas

Peninsula

ECONOMIC CYPRUS

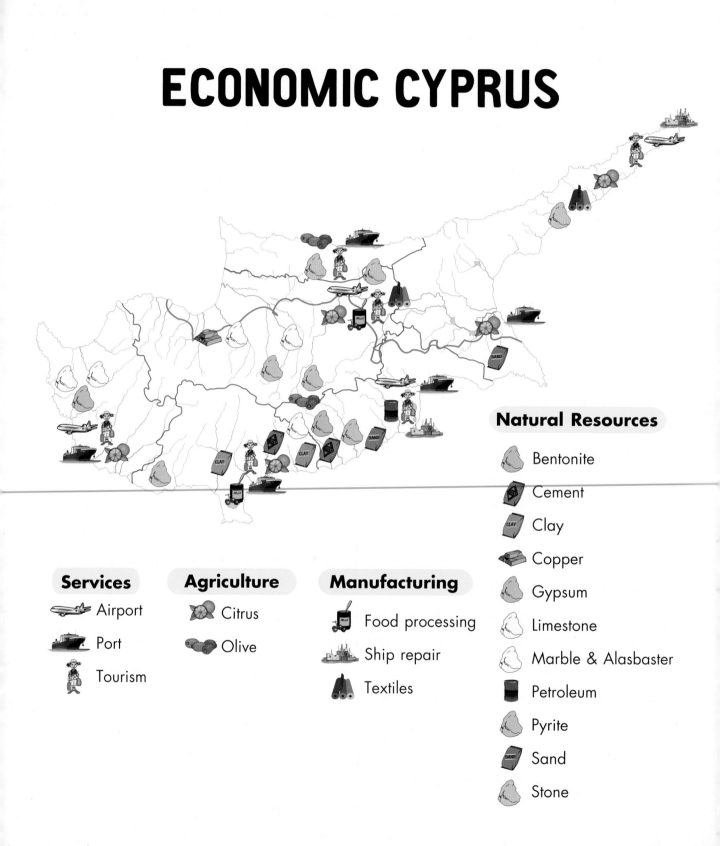

Services

- ✈ Airport
- ⚓ Port
- 🧳 Tourism

Agriculture

- 🍊 Citrus
- 🫒 Olive

Manufacturing

- 🥫 Food processing
- 🚢 Ship repair
- Textiles

Natural Resources

- Bentonite
- Cement
- Clay
- Copper
- Gypsum
- Limestone
- Marble & Alasbaster
- Petroleum
- Pyrite
- Sand
- Stone

ABOUT THE ECONOMY

OVERVIEW

Area under government control:

Cyprus adopted the Euro as its national currency on January 1, 2008. The service sector accounts for 78.3 percent of GDP. Cyprus today has a strong economy, although growth rate can fluctuate due to its overreliance on tourism. As a result of the global economic crisis in 2009, Cyprus's prosperity has suffered, as construction and tourism slow in the face of reduced foreign demand.

Turkish Cyprus:

The Turkish Cypriot economy has approximately 40 percent of the per capita GDP of the south. About half of the workforce is employed in agriculture and services. GDP declined by about 2.0 percent in 2007. The Turkish Cypriots are heavily dependent on investment from the Turkish government, which finances about 30 percent of the TRNC's budget. Aid from Turkey has exceeded $400 million annually in recent years.

CURRENCY

Area under government control: 1 U.S. dollar = 0.6827 Euros (EUR) (2008 estimate), 1 U.S. dollar = 0.4286 Cypriot pounds (2007 estimate); Turkish Cyprus: 1 U.S. dollar = 1.319 Turkish new lira (2007)

GROSS DOMESTIC PRODUCT (GDP)

$25.59 billion (2008 estimate)

GDP PER CAPITA

Area under government control: $28,600 (2008 estimate); Turkish Cyprus: $11,700 (2007 estimate)

GROWTH RATE

Area under government control: 3.6 percent (2008 estimate); Turkish Cyprus: -2 percent (2007 estimate)

GDP BY SECTOR

Area under government control: Agriculture: 2.6; percent industry: 19.1 percent; services: 78.3 percent (2008 estimate); Turkish Cyprus: Agriculture: 8.6 percent industry: 22.5 percent services: 69.1 percent (2006 estimate)

UNEMPLOYMENT RATE

Area under government control: 3.8 percent (2008 estimate); Turkish Cyprus: 9.4 percent (2005 estimate)

MAIN TRADE PARTNERS

Area under government control: Greece 21.1 percent; UK 14.3 percent; Germany 6.6 percent (2007); Turkish Cyprus: Turkey 40 percent; direct trade between Turkish Cyprus and the area under government control remains limited

MAIN EXPORTS

Area under government control: Citrus, potatoes, pharmaceuticals, cement, and clothing; Turkish Cyprus: Citrus, dairy, potatoes, textiles

CULTURAL CYPRUS

The Tombs of the Kings
A UNESCO World Heritage Site, the "Tombs of the Kings" are situated close to the sea in the northwestern necropolis of Paphos. They owe their name to their size and splendour and not because royalty was buried there. They are rock cut and date to the Hellenistic and early Roman periods. Some of them imitate the houses of the living, with the rooms (here the burial chambers) opening onto a peristyle atrium.

Chorokoita
Inscribed as a UNESCO World Heritage Site in 1998, the Neolithic settlement of Choirokoitia in the district of Larnaca, occupied from the 7th to the 4th millennium B.C., is one of the most important prehistoric sites in the eastern Mediterranean. Since only part of the site has been excavated, it forms an exceptional archaeological reserve for future study.

Kyrenia and Kyrenia Castle
Kyrenia was founded in the 10th century B.C., by Achaean settlers and was for many centuries one of the ten kingdoms of Cyprus. The town remained a minor port under Ottoman rule. Under British rule, the harbor and quay were built. The impressive Kyrenia Castle, at the eastern end of the harbor, was built in the 7th century by the Byzantines in order to protect the city against Arab raids. Just behind the harbor is the Agha Cafer Pasha mosque, constructed in 1580 during the Ottoman period. Beside the mosque lies the Hasan Kavizade Huseyin Efendi fountain, built in 1841.

Nicosia
Nicosia lies roughly at the center of the island and is the only capital city in the world to remain divided by force. It has a rich history that can be traced back to the Bronze Age. It is a magnificent city with a Royal Palace and over fifty churches. Today it blends its historic past brilliantly with the bustle of a modern city. The old walled city, enclosed by 16th-century Venetian walls, is dotted with museums, ancient churches, and medieval buildings.

Painted Churches in the Troodos Region
Inscribed as a UNESCO World Heritage Site in 1985, this Troodos region in the districts of Nicosia and Limassol is characterized by one of the largest groups of churches and monasteries of the former Byzantine Empire. The complex of 10 monuments all richly decorated with murals, provides an overview of Byzantine and post-Byzantine painting.

Famagusta, Salamis, and Enkomi
Famagusta possesses the deepest harbor and is one of the most fortified ports in the Mediterranean. Nearby are two ancient towns, Enkomi and Salamis. Enkomi was one of the first settlements in eastern Cyprus. The spectacular ruins at Salamis include a magnificent amphitheater, Roman baths, gymnasium, and royal tombs.

Maa-Palaeokastro Settlement
Maa-Palaeokastro is a settlement on the western coast of the island close to Coral Bay. Its imposing defensive walls were always exposed and gave the site its name of "Palaeokastro" ("the old castle"). This area was settled by the first Mycenaean Greeks who arrived on the island around 1200 B.C., after the fall of the Mycenaean kingdoms in mainland Greece. The site is well known for its fortification walls.

Paphos
Paphos is situated along the southwestern coast. It is the mythical birthplace of Aphrodite, the Greek goddess of love and beauty. In Greco-Roman times Paphos was the island's capital, and it is famous for the remains of the Roman governor's palace, where extensive, beautiful mosaics can be found. The town is included in the official UNESCO World Heritage list.

Limassol
Limassol is situated in the south of the island. It is Cyprus's main industrial and maritime area and also the second-largest town of the country. Places of interest include the old city; Berengaria Castle, the place where Richard the Lionheart married Berengaria; Kolossi Castle; the ancient city of Curium and its still functioning theater, Amathunta; and many other archeological spots scattered around the city.

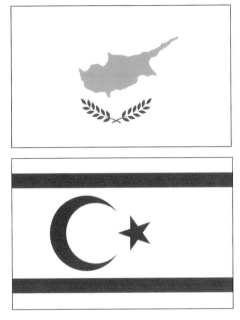

NATIONALITY
Cypriot, Turkish Cypriot

CAPITAL
Nicosia (Lefkoşa)

LAND AREA
3,568 square miles (9,240 sq km)

POPULATION
796,740 (July 2009 estimate)

ADMINISTRATIVE DISTRICTS
6 districts; Famagusta, Kyrenia, Larnaca, Limassol, Nicosia, Paphos; Turkish Cypriot area's administrative divisions include Kyrenia, all but a small part of Famagusta, and small parts of Nicosia (Lefkosia)

LANGUAGES
Greek, Turkish, English

ETHNIC GROUPS
Greek 77 percent, Turkish 18 percent, other 5 percent (2001 census)

MAJOR RELIGIONS
Greek Orthodox 78 percent, Muslim 18 percent, other (includes Maronite and Armenian Apostolic) 4 percent

BIRTHRATE
12.57 births/1,000 population (2009 estimate)

INFANT MORTALITY RATE
6.6 deaths/1,000 live births

LIFE EXPECTANCY
78.33 years; male: 75.91 years; female: 80.86 years (2009 estimate)

OFFICIAL NAME
Republic of Cyprus
The Turkish Cypriot community refers to itself as the Turkish Republic of Northern Cyprus (TRNC).

NATIONAL FLAG
White with a copper-colored silhouette of the island above two green crossed olive branches that symbolize the hope for peace and reconciliation between the Greek and Turkish communities.

The Turkish Republic of Northern Cyprus flag has a white field with narrow horizontal red stripes a small distance from the top and bottom edges, with a red crescent and a red five-pointed star in the middle.

TIME LINE

IN CYPRUS	IN THE WORLD

8th century B.C.
Cyprus conquered and unified by the
Assyrian Empire under Sargon II.

285 B.C.
Ptolemy II of Macedonia rules Egypt and
founds the Cypriot port of Famagusta.

116–17 B.C.
The Roman Empire reaches its greatest extent,
under Emperor Trajan (98–17).

878
The British military occupy and administer
Cyprus by mutual agreement with the
Ottoman government.

1206–1368
Genghis Khan unifies the Mongols and starts
conquest of the world. At its height, the Mongol
Empire under Kublai Khan stretches from China
to Persia and parts of Europe and Russia.

1530
Beginning of transatlantic slave trade organized
by the Portuguese in Africa.

1789–99
The French Revolution

1914
World War I begins.

1925
Cyprus becomes a British Crown colony.

1931
Violent protests by Greek Cypriots
demanding union with mainland Greece.

1939
World War II begins.

1945
The United States drops atomic bombs on
Hiroshima and Nagasaki. World War II ends.

1955
National Organization of Cypriot Fighters
(EOKA), Greek Cypriot activists and guerrilla
fighters, begin a bombing campaign to
support their push for union with Greece.

1958
Turkish Cypriots, alarmed by British
conciliation, begin demands for partition.

IN CYPRUS	IN THE WORLD

1960
Cyprus becomes independent.
Archbishop Makarios becomes the first
president, with Turkish Cypriot Dr. Kutchuk
as vice president.

1966
The Chinese Cultural Revolution.

1963
Interethnic fighting erupts after political
disagreements.

1974
Makarios is overthrown in a military
backed coup. Turkey invades the north. The
coup is put down and Makarios returned to
power. After talks break down, Turkey lands
40,000 troops in the north, occupying 37
percent of the island. Turkish Cypriots living in
the south move to the Turkish occupied north.

1983
The north declares itself an independent
state, the Turkish Republic of Northern
Cyprus (TRNC).

1986
Nuclear power disaster at Chernobyl in
Ukraine.

1991
Breakup of the Soviet Union.

1997
Hong Kong is returned to China.

2001
Terrorists crash planes in New York,
Washington D.C., and Pennsylvania.

2004
Cyprus is admitted to the European Union.

2006
UN-sponsored talks between the north
and south result in the agreement of a series
of confidence-building measures.

2008
Dimitris Christofias becomes Cyprus's first
Communist president.

2008
Earthquake in Sichuan province, China, kills
thousands.

2009
Right-wing nationalist National Unity
Party wins parliamentary elections in northern
Cyprus, potentially hampering peace talks.

GLOSSARY

affedersiniz (ahf-ehd-ehr-sih-NIH Z)
Means "sorry" or "I beg your pardon."

aïráni (ah-ee-RAHN -ee)
A refreshing concoction of diluted yogurt mixed with dried mint or oregano.

bilgi (bihl-GEE)
Means knowledge.

bir dakika (bih dah-kih-KAH)
Means "wait a minute."

cepken (chep-KEHN)
Short, embroidered vests worn by Turkish Cypriot men.

dhrepanin (threh-PAH -neen)
Means "sickle dance."

enosis
A Greek word meaning "unification."

Fóta
The Greek name for the Orthodox celebration of the Epiphany in January.

karpasitiko (karp-ahs-IHT -ih-koh)
Popular traditional dress worn by Greek Cypriot women.

kartchilamas (gar-chee-LAH -mahs)
A popular Cypriot dance performed by facing pairs of male and female dancers.

Kurban Bayrami
Muslim Feast of the Sacrifice.

laoudo (LAH -oo-doh)
A long-necked flute.

misafir (mihs-ah-FEER)
Turkish word for "guest."

ne haber (neh hah-BER)
Means "how are you."

pitharia (PIH -thah-ree-ah)
Large, traditional Cypriot earthenware containers used for storing olives, wine, and olive oil.

pó-pó-pó (POH -poh-poh)
Expression of dismay.

Seker Bayrami
The Muslim feast celebrating the end of the fasting month of Ramadan. *Seker Bayrami* means "sugar festival."

shalvar (shaht-VAH R)
Baggy trousers worn by Turkish Cypriot men and women.

sigá sigá (see-GAH see-GAH)
Means "slow down and relax."

syrtos (SEE -tohs) and **mandra (MAHN -drah)**
Complicated dances.

taksim (tahk-SIH M)
A Turkish word meaning "partition."

ti néa (tee NEH -ah)
Means "what's new."

yá sou (YA soo)
Means "health to you."

FOR FURTHER INFORMATION

BOOKS

Cyprus (DK Eyewitness Travel Guide). London, UK: Dorling Kindersley, 2008.

Dubin, Mark. *The Rough Guide to Cyprus*. London, UK: Rough Guides Publishing,. 2009.

Gursoy, K. and Neville Smith, L. *Northern Cyprus* (Landmark Visitors Guide). London, UK: Landmark Publishing Ltd., 2009.

Mallinson, William. *Cyprus: A Modern History*. London, UK: I. B. Tauris & Co Ltd., 2008.

Maric, Vesna. *Cyprus* (Lonely Planet Country Guide). Hawthorn, Vic. ; Oakland, CA: Lonely Planet Publications, 2006.

WEBSITES

news.bbc.co.uk/2/hi/europe/country_profiles/1021835.stm

www.birdlifecyprus.org

www.cia.gov/library/publications/the-world-factbook/geos/cy.html

www.cypenv.org

www.cyprus.gov.cy

www.cyprusweekly.com

www.environmentalgrafitti.com

www.euro.who.int/eehc/implementation/20050527_2

www.kypros.org/Cyprus/environment.html

www.nationsencyclopedia.com

www.unicef.org/infobycountry/cyprus.html

www.un.org/Depts/dpko/missions/unficyp

www.windowoncyprus.com/politics.htm

FILMS

Ian Cross, *Globe Trekker: Cyprus and Crete*, 2008.

Michael Cacoyannis, *Attila 74: The Rape Of Cyprus*, 1975.

MUSIC

Cyprien Katsaris, *A Tribute to Cyprus*, Piano 21, 2000.

Various Artists, *Air Mail Music Series: Cyprus—Tradition*, Airmail, 2008.

Various Artists, *Music of Northern Cyprus*, Arc, 2006.

Various Artists, *Folk Music of Greece & Cyprus*, Lyrichord, 1999.

BIBLIOGRAPHY

www.blnz.com/news/2009/04/24/Cyprus_tourism_revenues_slide_128_0683.html
www.centralbank.gov.cy/nqcontent.cfm?a_id=1130&lang=en
www.hospitalitynet.org/news/4040612.search?query=tourism+revenue+cyprus
www.mof.gov.cy/mof/cystat/statistics.nsf/All/9F1C23E6FFC9439DC22575CC0031258
   7?OpenDocument&sub=1&e=`

INDEX

INDEX